TOWARD
A MORE RESPONSIBLE
TWO-PARTY SYSTEM

A Report

OF THE COMMITTEE ON POLITICAL PARTIES
AMERICAN POLITICAL SCIENCE ASSOCIATION

New York · 1950 · *Toronto*

RINEHART & COMPANY, INC.

This material appeared as a *Supplement*
to *The American Political Science Review*,
Vol. XLIV, No. 3, Part 2, September, 1950.

FOREWORD

This is the proper place to answer four questions: What is the purpose of this publication? What is its thesis? How were its conclusions arrived at? And on whose authority are they offered?

The *purpose* of this publication is to bring about fuller public appreciation of a basic weakness in the American two-party system. In other words, this is not a research document aimed at professional readers only. It seeks the attention of every one interested in politics. It is therefore written without regard for the customary form in which scholars present their scientific findings. It does not line up and evaluate every pertinent fact. It sums up the main facts.

At the same time, this publication is a summation of professional knowledge. Its authors are students of politics. Each has previously examined in separate studies various aspects of the broad subject here discussed. Although this is a summation of knowledge, it rests on the results of scientific analysis that have come from the research activity of a great number of specialists.

Of course, if the American two-party system suffers from a basic weakness, the most important thing is effective remedy. Remedy requires not only understanding of the ailment but also willingness to try a likely cure. Both understanding and willingness, in turn, must be fairly widespread. It is not enough for a few people to know about ailment and cure. Before action has a chance, knowledge must first become sufficiently common. The character of this publication is explained by the conviction of its authors that the weakness of the American two-party system can be overcome as soon as a substantial part of the electorate wants it overcome. Hence it is essential to reach the ears of many citizens.

And the *thesis?* It can be put quite briefly. Historical and other factors have caused the American two-party system to operate as two loose associations of state and local organizations, with very little national machinery and very little national cohesion. As a result, either major party, when in power, is ill-equipped to organize its members in the legislative and the executive branches into a government held together and guided by the party program. Party responsibility at the polls thus tends to vanish. This is a very serious matter, for it affects the very heartbeat of American democracy. It also poses grave problems of domestic and foreign policy in an era when it is no longer safe for the nation to deal piecemeal with issues that can be disposed of only on the basis of coherent programs.

Can anything be done about it? Yes, a good many things can be done about it. In presenting suggestions, however, this publication confines itself to showing concrete lines of approach. Its authors do not believe in panaceas. Nor do they believe that organizational and procedural rearrangements by themselves work lasting changes. Real change comes from an appreciation of its need, by ordinary citizens as well as by political leaders. Such proposals for readjustment of the party machinery as are offered here are meant to meet the perfectly sensible complaint that purely negative criticism is of little use.

In *arriving at the conclusions* embodied in this publication, its authors have relied upon the methods of analysis they are familiar with through their training and work as political scientists. Though scientific knowledge about the American party system is by no means complete, it was found practicable here to build upon available data and insights. The most important thing appeared to be to present the available knowledge in the perspective of its principal inferences.

To this end, the authors, working together over almost four years as the Committee on Political Parties of the American Political Science Association, have gathered ideas and information in various ways. They have written and exchanged a considerable number of professional papers and memoranda on individual parts of the large subject before them. They have sought and obtained professional contributions and recommendations from other political scientists with specialized knowledge. They have consulted with many people engaged practically in different segments of the political process, both individually and in special sessions as far apart as New York and Seattle. And they have held open and closed meetings for the purpose of joint consideration of difficult problems and crystallization of conclusions. A conscientious effort has been made to get hold of every strand of thinking on the American two-party system.

In approaching its task in this way, the Committee on Political Parties was necessarily influenced by the degree of financial support it was able to secure for its activity. Initially, it had been hoped to obtain funds for an extensive fresh study of a subject as vital to democratic government as the party system. These hopes proved futile. As a result, the Committee on Political Parties had to live on a shoestring. The American Political Science Association made available a sum of money, which covered the larger part of the Committee's travel and duplicating costs. Without this grant the Committee could hardly have begun to take up its work. Even so some of the essential costs had to be met out of the pockets of individual members and to some extent by the institutions they are serving.

This publication has gone through several stages and more than one draft. A fairly complete preliminary draft, based upon the work done during the preceding years, was finally developed in the spring of 1950. The preliminary draft was circulated widely among men and women whose knowledge of the political process the Committee was eager to bring to bear upon the emerging report. These included members of Congress, staff assistants to legislators, civic leaders, legislative representatives of interest groups, members of the press, officers and staff aides in the executive agencies, experts associated with private research foundations and teachers of political science. The preliminary draft was also taken up with the National Committees of the two major parties.

Valuable comments on the preliminary draft were received formally and informally from various party officials as well as from individual members of Congress. Congressman Joseph W. Martin, Jr., Minority Leader of the House of Representatives, was especially generous in giving the Committee the benefit of his great experience. The Committee owes a similar debt to members of the staff of the President.

A complete list of all those to whom the Committee is indebted for counsel and criticism in improving the preliminary draft would take much space. Here it must suffice to name only some of those who have been particularly helpful. They include: William Anderson, University of Minnesota; Stephen K. Bailey, Wesleyan University; Louis Bean, Department of Agriculture; Donald C. Blaisdell, Department of State; Richard S. Childs, National Municipal League; Kenneth Colegrove, Northwestern University; Edwin A. Cottrell, Haynes Foundation; Frederick M. Davenport, Federal Personnel Council; John A. Davis, Lincoln University; H. Schuyler Foster, Department of State; George B. Galloway, Library of Congress; Joseph P. Harris, University of California; Arthur N. Holcombe, Harvard University; Avery Leiserson, University of Chicago; Norton E. Long, Western Reserve University; Lewis Meriam, Brookings Institution; Charles E. Merriam, University of Chicago; Harold W. Metz, Brookings Institution; Don K. Price, Public Administration Clearing House; Floyd M. Riddick, Congressional Daily Digest; Lloyd M. Short, University of Minnesota; Harold Stein, Committee on Public Administration Cases; and John A. Vieg, Pomona College.

The Committee owes a special debt of gratitude to James K. Pollock, University of Michigan, and Peter H. Odegard, University of California, for their strong support of the Committee's work as President and President-Elect, respectively, of the American Political Science Association. Thanks are also due Taylor Cole, Duke University, who as Managing Editor of the AMERICAN POLITICAL SCIENCE REVIEW undertook to have this report printed and distributed as a supplement to the fall issue.

Finally, *whose voice is heard* in this publication? Its conclusions stand solely on the professional judgment of the members of the Committee on Political Parties. The American Political Science Association, with its large membership, does not put itself on record as a body behind findings agreed upon among groups of political scientists, including its own committees. The American Political Science Association, through its chosen organs, has approved the publication of this report as the work of its Committee on Political Parties. Such approval means no formal endorsement of the substance of the report.

And who are the members of the Committee on Political Parties? They are: Thomas S. Barclay, Stanford University; Clarence A. Berdahl, University of Illinois; Hugh A. Bone, University of Washington; Franklin L. Burdette, University of Maryland; Paul T. David, Brookings Institution; Merle Fainsod, Harvard University; Bertram M. Gross, Council of Economic Advisers; E. Allen Helms, Ohio State University; E. M. Kirkpatrick, Department of State; John W. Lederle, University of Michigan; Fritz Morstein Marx, American University; Louise Overacker, Wellesley College; Howard Penniman, Department of State; Kirk H. Porter, State University of Iowa; J. B. Shannon, University of Kentucky; and E. E. Schattschneider, Wesleyan University, as chairman.

The drafting committee was composed of: Clarence A. Berdahl, Bertram M. Gross, Louise Overacker, E. E. Schattschneider, and Fritz Morstein Marx, as chairman.

How does a committee of this kind get under way? To make a long story short, the Committee on Political Parties was organized on the model of an earlier committee of the American Political Science Association, the Committee on Congress. This committee, under the chairmanship of George B. Galloway, had made a large and widely acknowledged contribution toward the strengthening of Congress and the passage in 1946 of the Legislative Reorganization Act. On the other hand, the efforts of the Committee on Congress had dealt only indirectly with the party system. It was therefore logical to raise the question of further ways and means of increasing the Federal Government's capacity for coping effectively with the momentous problems of our times. The more thought was given to this question, the clearer became the pivotal character of the party system.

On the strength of these considerations, the American Political Science Association created the Committee on Political Parties at its annual meeting in Cleveland in December, 1946. From the outset, however, it was made quite explicit that the new committee should center its attention on the condition and improvement of *national* party organization. This emphasis has governed the work of the Committee from its inception. The same emphasis is manifest in the Committee's report.

In presenting this report, the Committee on Political Parties is impressed with its own limitations, with the areas that have remained inadequately illuminated, and with the rich opportunities for research that challenge the imagination of the student of political parties. It is gratifying that the work of the Committee has not only aroused much new interest but also proved useful as a stepping stone for several recent contributions to the literature on the American party system. Nothing would be more satisfying to the whole committee membership than to know that its report has served as a starting point for constructive public debate, creative political action, and more intensive scientific studies.

August, 1950

CONTENTS

SUMMARY OF CONCLUSIONS AND PROPOSALS

PART I. THE NEED FOR GREATER PARTY RESPONSIBILITY

1. *The Role of the Political Parties*

1. *The Parties and Public Policy.* Popular government in a nation of more than 150 million people requires political parties which provide the electorate with a proper range of choice between alternatives of action. In order to keep the parties apart, one must consider the relations between each and public policy. The reasons for the growing emphasis on public policy in party politics are to be found, above all, in the very operations of modern government.

2. *The New Importance of Program.* The crux of public affairs lies in the necessity for more effective formulation of general policies and programs and for better integration of all of the far-flung activities of modern government. It is in terms of party programs that political leaders can attempt to consolidate public attitudes toward the work plans of government.

3. *The Potentialities of the Party System.* The potentialities of the two-party system are suggested, on the one hand, by the fact that for all practical purposes the major parties monopolize elections; and, on the other, by the fact that both parties have in the past managed to adapt themselves to the demands made upon them by external necessities. It is good practical politics to reconsider party organization in the light of the changing conditions of politics. Happily such an effort entails an application of ideas about the party system that are no longer unfamiliar.

2. *What Kind of Party System Is Needed?*

The party system that is needed must be democratic, responsible and effective.

I. A Stronger Two-party System

1. *The Need for an Effective Party System.* An effective party system requires, first, that the parties are able to bring forth programs to which they commit themselves and, second, that the parties possess sufficient internal cohesion to carry out these programs. Such a degree of unity within the parties cannot be brought about without party procedures that give a large body of people an opportunity to share in the development of the party program.

2. *The Need for an Effective Opposition Party.* The fundamental requirement of accountability is a two-party system in which the opposition party acts as the critic of the party in power, developing, defining

1

and presenting the policy alternatives which are necessary for a true choice in reaching public decisions. The opposition most conducive to responsible government is an organized party opposition.

II. Better Integrated Parties

1. *The Need for a Party System with Greater Resistance to Pressure.* There is little to suggest that the phenomenal growth of interest organizations in recent decades has come to its end. The whole development makes necessary a reinforced party system that can cope with the multiplied organized pressures. Compromise among interests is compatible with the aims of a free society only when the terms of reference reflect an openly acknowledged concept of the public interest.

2. *The Need for a Party System with Sufficient Party Loyalty.* Needed clarification of party policy will not cause the parties to differ more fundamentally or more sharply than they have in the past. Nor is it to be assumed that increasing concern with their programs will cause the parties to erect between themselves an ideological wall. Parties have the right and the duty to announce the terms to govern participation in the common enterprise. The emphasis in all consideration of party discipline must be on positive measures to create a strong and general agreement on policies. A basis for party cohesion in Congress will be established as soon as the parties interest themselves sufficiently in their congressional candidates to set up strong and active campaign organizations in the constituencies.

III. More Responsible Parties

1. *The Need for Parties Responsible to the Public.* Party responsibility means the responsibility of both parties to the general public, as enforced in elections. Party responsibility to the public, enforced in elections, implies that there be more than one party, for the public can hold a party responsible only if it has a choice. As a means of achieving responsibility, the clarification of party policy also tends to keep public debate on a more realistic level, restraining the inclination of party spokesmen to make unsubstantiated statements and charges.

2. *The Need for Parties Responsible to Their Members.* Party responsibility includes also the responsibility of party leaders to the party membership, as enforced in primaries, caucuses and conventions. The external and the internal kinds of party responsibility need not conflict. Intraparty conflict will be minimized if it is generally recognized that national, state and local party leaders have a common responsibility to the party membership. National party leaders have a legitimate interest in the nomination of congressional candidates.

3. *The Inadequacy of the Existing Party System*

I. Beginning Transition

1. *Change and Self-examination.* Marked changes in the structure and processes of American society have necessarily affected the party system. The prevailing climate of self-examination as well as the current tendencies toward change in the party system give point to inquiries like that represented by our report.

2. *Burden of the Past.* Formal party organization in its main features is still substantially what it was before the Civil War. Under these circumstances the main trends of American politics have tended to outflank the party system.

II. Some Basic Problems

1. *The Federal Basis.* The two parties are organized on a federal basis. The national and state party organizations are largely independent of one another, without appreciable common approach to problems of party policy and strategy. The real issue is not over the federal form of organization but over the right balance of forces within this type of organization. A corollary of the kind of federalism now expressed in the party system is an excessive measure of internal separatism.

2. *The Location of Leadership.* Party organization does not vest leadership of the party as a whole in either a single person or a committee. There is at present no central figure or organ which could claim authority to take up party problems, policies and strategy.

3. *The Ambiguity of Membership.* No understandings or rules or criteria exist with respect to membership in a party. Those who suggest that elections should deal with personalities but not with programs suggest at the same time that party membership should mean nothing at all.

III. Specific Deficiencies

1. *National Party Organs.* The National Convention, as at present constituted and operated, is an unwieldy, unrepresentative and less than responsible body. The National Committee is seldom a generally influential body and much less a working body. House and Senate campaign committees do not always have a good working relationship with the National Committee. Although interest in questions of party policy has grown, the national party organs are not so constituted nor so coordinated as to make it simple for them to pay enough attention to these questions.

2. *Party Platforms.* Alternatives between the parties are defined so badly that it is often difficult to determine what the election has decided

even in broadest terms. The prevailing procedure for the writing and adoption of national party platforms is too hurried and too remote from the process by which actual decisions are made to command the respect of the whole party and the electorate. The platform should be the end product of a long search for a working agreement within the party.

3. *Intraparty Democracy.* Too little consideration has been given to ways and means of bringing about a constructive relationship between the party and its members. In making the most of popular participation, the performance of American parties is very unsatisfactory.

4. *Party Research.* A party stands as much in need of research as does business enterprise or the government itself.

4. *New Demands upon Party Leadership*
I. The Nature of Modern Public Policy

1. *Broad Range of Policy.* The expanding responsibilities of modern government have brought about so extensive an interlacing of governmental action with the country's economic and social life that the need for coordinated and coherent programs, legislative as well as administrative, has become paramount. In a democracy no general program can be adopted and carried out without wide public support.

2. *Impact on the Public.* In a predominantly industrial society, public policy tends to be widely inclusive, involving in its objectives and effects very large segments of the public or even the whole country.

3. *Governmental Program Machinery.* On the side of government, in the administrative and the legislative spheres, the twin needs for program formulation and for program machinery have long been recognized. The governmental advance toward program formulation needs now to be paralleled in the political sphere proper—above all, in the party system.

II. Rise of Nation-wide Policy Issues

1. *An Historic Trend.* The changes in the nature and scope of public policy are the result of changes in the social structure and in the economy of the United States.

2. *Past and Present Factors.* There has been in recent decades a continuing decline of sectionalism. Party organization designed to deal with the increasing volume of national issues must give wide range to the national party leadership.

3. *New Interest Groups in Politics.* The economic and social factors that have reduced the weight of sectionalism have also resulted in the development of a new type of interest groups, built upon large membership. To a much greater extent than in the past, they operate as if they were auxiliary organizations of one or the other party.

5. *The Question of Constitutional Amendment*

1. *A Cabinet System?* A responsible cabinet system makes the leaders of the majority collectively accountable for the conduct of the government.

2. *Strong Parties as a Condition.* To amend the Constitution in order to create a responsible cabinet system is not a practicable way of getting more effective parties.

3. *Adaptation Within the Constitution.* The parties can do much to adapt the usages under the Constitution to their purposes.

PART II. PROPOSALS FOR PARTY RESPONSIBILITY

6. *National Party Organization*

I. Principal Party Bodies

1. *The National Convention.* We assume its continuation as the principal representative and deliberative organ of the party. The convention should meet at least biennially, with easy provision for special meetings. It should also cease to be a delegate convention of unwieldy size.

2. *The National Committee.* It is highly desirable for the National Convention to reassert its authority over the National Committee through a more active participation in the final selection of the committee membership. It is also desirable that the members of the National Committee reflect the actual strength of the party within the areas they represent.

3. *The Party Council.* We propose a Party Council of 50 members. Such a Party Council should consider and settle the larger problems of party management, within limits prescribed by the National Convention; propose a preliminary draft of the party platform to the National Convention; interpret the platform in relation to current problems; choose for the National Convention the group of party leaders outside the party organizations; consider and make recommendations to appropriate party organs in respect to congressional candidates; and make recommendations to the National Convention, the National Committee or other appropriate party organs with respect to conspicuous departures from general party decisions by state or local party organizations. In presidential years, the council would naturally become a place for the discussion of presidential candidacies, and might well perform the useful function of screening these candidacies in a preliminary way. Within this Party Council there might well be a smaller group of party advisers to serve as a party cabinet.

II. Intraparty Relationships

1. *State and Local Party Organizations.* Organizational patterns of the parties are predicated on the assumption that a party committee is necessary for each electoral area. There is a growing dissatisfaction with the results of this system on the local level, especially the multiplicity of organizations. An increasing number of state legislators are noting the breakdown or lack of party responsibility and discipline and the growth of internal separatism in state government. It is necessary for both parties to reexamine their purposes and functions in the light of the present-day environment, state and local, in which they operate.

2. *Relations between National, State and Local Organizations.* Establishment of a Party Council would do much to coordinate the different party organizations, and should be pressed with that objective in mind. Regional conferences held by both parties have clearly been fruitful. Regional party organizations should be encouraged. Local party organizations should be imbued with a stronger sense of loyalty to the entire party organization and feel their responsibility for promoting the broader policies of the party. This can be done by fostering local party meetings, regularly and frequently held, perhaps monthly. The national organization may deal with conspicuous or continued disloyalty on the part of any state organization. Consideration should be given to the development of additional means of dealing with rebellious and disloyal state organizations.

3. *Headquarters and Staff.* Both parties are now aware of the need to maintain permanent headquarters, with staff equipped for research and publicity. A beginning has been made, but much still remains to be done. Staff development at party headquarters provides the essential mechanism to enable each party to concern itself appropriately with its continuing responsibilities.

7. *Party Platforms*

I. Nature of the Platform

1. *Alternative Purposes.* Should the party platform be a statement of general principles representing the permanent or long-range philosophy of the party? Or should it state the party's position on immediate issues? Actually, the platform is usually made up of both the more permanent and the more fleeting elements.

2. *Interpretation of the Platform.* As a body representing the various parts of the party structure, the Party Council should be able to give authoritative and reasonably acceptable interpretations of the platform.

3. *National-state Platform Conflicts.* What is needed is better coordi-

nation in the declaration of party principles. The Party Council would be the appropriate party agency to interpret the respective platforms and determine the right position in case of conflict. There is very little likelihood indeed for the Party Council to be inconsiderate of arguable claims of state autonomy.

4. *Binding Character.* In spite of clear implications and express pledges, there has been much difference of opinion as to the exact binding quality of a platform. All of this suggests the need for appropriate machinery, such as a Party Council, to interpret and apply the national program in respect to doubts or details. When that is done by way of authoritative and continuing statement, the party program should be considered generally binding.

II. Problems of Platform-making

1. *Method of Formulating Party Platforms.* Occasionally the state platforms are deliberately delayed until after the national platform has been adopted, in order to have a basis for conformity. Such practice is to be encouraged, and state legislation that prevents it ought to be changed. A method of platform-making that is closely related to the congressional as well as to the presidential campaign must be developed, and with more direct participation by the party members of Congress.

2. *Improvement of Platforms and Platform-making.* In both parties, the Platform Committee or a working part of it is now appointed some weeks in advance of the National Convention. The practice of holding public hearings on the policies to be incorporated into the platform has been fairly well established. This consultation is of importance, for it makes the parties aware of the interest in particular policies.

3. *Proposals.* Party platforms should be formulated at least every two years. National platforms should emphasize general party principles and national issues. State and local platforms should be expected to conform to the national platform on matters of general party principle or on national policies. To achieve better machinery for platform-making, the Party Council, when set up, should prepare a tentative draft well in advance of the National Convention for the consideration of the appropriate convention committee and the convention itself. Local party meetings should be held for the discussion and consideration of platform proposals.

8. *Party Organization in Congress*

I. Introduction

1. *External Factors.* A higher degree of party responsibility in Congress cannot be provided merely by actions taken within Congress. Nevertheless, action within Congress can be of decisive significance.

2. *Continuous Evolution.* The materials for responsible party operations in Congress are already on hand. The key to progress lies in making a full-scale effort to use them.

II. Tightening Up the Congressional Party Organization

1. *The Leaders.* For more than ten years now the press has carried news about regular meetings between the President and the Big Four of Congress—the Speaker of the House, the Majority Leader of the House, the Vice President and the Majority Leader of the Senate, when the four are of the President's party. It would be an error to attempt to supplant the relationship between the Big Four and the President by some new body. Whenever it becomes necessary for the President to meet with the leaders of both parties in Congress, it is a simple matter for the Big Four to be expanded to six or eight. In the public eye a party leader like these is a spokesman for his party as a whole. It is necessary that there be broad consultation throughout the national leadership of a party before a party leader is elected in either house.

2. *The Leadership Committees.* We submit these proposals: In both the Senate and the House, the various leadership groups should be consolidated into one truly effective and responsible leadership committee for each party. Each of these four committees should be responsible not only for submitting policy proposals to the party membership, but also for discharging certain functions with respect to the committee structure and the legislative schedule. Each of the four committees should be selected or come up for a vote of confidence no less often than every two years. Occasion must be found reasonably often for the leadership committees of each party in the two houses to meet together. Furthermore, the rival leadership committees in each house should meet together on a more regular basis. A case can also be made for the four leadership groups to meet on specific occasions.

3. *Caucuses or Conferences.* More frequent meetings of the party membership in each house should be held. A binding caucus decision on legislative policy should be used primarily to carry out the party's principles and program. When members of Congress disregard a caucus decision taken in furtherance of national party policy, they should expect disapproval. The party leadership committees should be responsible for calling more frequent caucuses or conferences and developing the agenda of points for discussion.

III. Party Responsibility for Committee Structure

1. *Selection of Committee Chairmen.* It is not playing the game fairly for party members who oppose the commitments in their party's platform to rely on seniority to carry them into committee chairmanships.

Party leaders have compelling reason to prevent such a member from becoming chairman—and they are entirely free so to exert their influence. The task of party leaders, when confronted with revolt on the part of committee chairmen, is not easy. Obviously problems of this sort must be handled in the electoral process itself as well as in the congressional arena.

2. *Assignment of Members to Committees.* The slates of committee assignments should be drawn up by the party leadership committees and presented to the appropriate party caucuses for approval or modification. There is nothing sound in having the party ratio on the committees always correspond closely to the party ratio in the House itself. Committee assignments should be subjected to regular reexamination by the party caucus or conference with reasonable frequency.

3. *Committee Staff.* Staff assistance should be available to minority as well as majority members of a committee whenever they want it. Where all committee staff is controlled by the majority, a change in power threatens continuity of service.

IV. Party Responsibility for the Legislative Schedule

1. *The Need for Scheduling.* Schedules should be openly explained on the floor in advance. No committee should be in charge of legislative scheduling except the party leadership committee.

2. *House Guidance of Legislative Traffic.* A democratic approach would be to substitute open party control for control by the Rules Committee or individual chairmen.

3. *The Right to Vote in the Senate.* The present cloture rule should be amended. The best rule is one that provides for majority cloture on all matters before the Senate.

9. *Political Participation*

Widespread political participation fosters responsibility as well as democratic control in the conduct of party affairs and the pursuit of party policies. A more responsible party system is intimately linked with the general level as well as the forms of political participation.

I. Intraparty Democracy

1. *Party Membership.* As stress is placed by the parties upon policy and the interrelationship of problems at various levels of government, association with a party should become more interesting and attractive to many who hold aloof today.

2. *Machinery of Intraparty Democracy.* If the National Convention is to serve as the grand assembly of the party, in which diverse viewpoints are compounded into a course of action, it must be nourished from

below. To this end local party groups are needed that meet frequently
to discuss and initiate policy.

3. *Toward a New Concept of Party Membership.* The existence of a
national program, drafted at frequent intervals by a party convention
both broadly representative and enjoying prestige, should make a great
difference. It would prompt those who identify themselves as Republicans or Democrats to think in terms of support of that program
rather than in terms of personalities, patronage and local matters.
Once machinery is established which gives the party member and his
representative a share in framing the party's objectives, once there are
safeguards against internal dictation by a few in positions of influence,
members and representatives will feel readier to assume an obligation
to support the program. Membership defined in these terms does not
ask for mindless discipline enforced from above. It generates self-discipline which stems from free identification with aims one helps to define.

II. Nominating Procedures

1. *United States Senator and Representative.* Nominations for United
States Senator and Representative are governed largely by state laws
that vary radically in their provisions. National regulation would
overcome the disadvantages of so much variety. But one must face
the practical objections to national regulation. The direct primary probably can be adapted to the needs of parties unified in terms of national
policy. The closed primary deserves preference because it is more readily
compatible with the development of a responsible party system. The
open primary tends to destroy the concept of membership as the basis
of party organization. Cross filing is bound to obscure program differences between the parties, and to eliminate any sense of real membership
on the part of the rank and file. The Washington blanket primary corrupts the meaning of party even further by permitting voters at the
same primary to roam at will among the parties. The formal or informal
proposal of candidates by preprimary meetings of responsible party
committees or party councils is a healthy development. Quite appropriately the Party Council might become a testing ground for candidates
for United States Senator or Representative.

2. *Presidential Nomination.* In the National Convention, delegates
representative of the party membership should be chosen by direct
vote of the rank and file. The Party Council naturally would concern
itself with platform plans and the relative claims of those who might be
considered for presidential and vice presidental nominations. In time
it may be feasible and desirable to substitute a direct, national presidential primary for the indirect procedure of the convention.

III. Elections

1. *Election of the President.* The present method of electing the President and Vice President fosters the blight of one-party monopoly and results in concentration of campaign artillery in pivotal industrial states where minority groups hold the balance of power. In the persistent agitation for change in the Electoral College system, stress should be placed both upon giving all sections of the country a real voice in electing the President and the Vice President and upon developing a two-party system in present one-party areas.

2. *Term of Representative.* It appears desirable to lengthen the term of Representatives to four years.

3. *Campaign Funds.* Existing statutory limitations work toward a scattering of responsibility for the collecting of funds among a large number of independent party and nonparty committees. Repeal of these restrictions would make it possible for a national body to assume more responsibility in the field of party finance. The situation might be improved in still another way by giving a specified measure of government assistance to the parties. Everything that makes the party system more meaningful to all voters leads incidentally to a broadening of the base of financial support of the parties.

4. *Apportionment and Redistricting.* It is time to insist upon congressional districts approximately equal in population.

IV. Barriers to Voting

1. *Registration.* The system of permanent registration should be extended. Properly qualified newcomers to an area should be permitted to register and vote without undue delay.

2. *Access to the Polls.* Legislation establishing National Election Day would in all probability bring to the polls large numbers of people who would otherwise never come. Holding elections on Saturdays or Sundays would probably also help to increase the size of the vote. Adequate voting time should be provided by opening the booths in the earlier morning hours and keeping them open into the late evening hours. There is room for much elaboration in laws governing absentee balloting.

3. *Undemocratic Limitations.* Intentionally limiting devices should be overcome by a combination of legal change and educational efforts. Action is indicated to extend the suffrage to the inhabitants of the District of Columbia.

4. *The Short Ballot.* Adoption of the short ballot would concentrate choice on contests with program implications and thus shift attention toward issues rather than personalities.

10. *Research on Political Parties*

I. Basic Facts and Figures

1. *Election Statistics.* We propose the publication of an election year-book by the Bureau of the Census. The arrangement of the yearbook should probably be by states. In addition, a summary booklet for presidential and congressional elections should be issued.

2. *Party Activities.* Compilation and regular publication of information on party activities are no less urgently needed.

3. *Compilation of Party Regulations.* A third task is the collection of all major regulations relating to national parties and elections.

II. More Research by the Parties

1. *Party Research Staffs.* What is needed is a stronger full-time research organization adequately financed and working on a year-in, year-out basis.

2. *Areas of Work.* There are two fields of research that should always be of immediate interest to the national organization of every party. The first is the analysis of voting trends and voting behavior. A second research field is analysis of proposals dealing with changes in election methods.

III. More Studies of the Parties

1. *Types of Research Needed.* In a field in which much still remains to be done, specific priorities have little meaning. The basic need is for a combination of creative hypotheses and realistic investigations.

2. *Professors and Politics.* The character of political research cannot be dissociated from the general approach of academic institutions to politics as a whole. Increased faculty participation in political affairs would mean more practical, realistic and useful teaching as well as research in the field of political parties.

3. *Role of Research Foundations.* The private foundations should actively solicit new ideas and proposals for research on political parties.

4. *Role of American Political Science Association.* The presentation of this report is but one instance of the interest shown in the subject of political parties by the American Political Science Association. In making specific suggestions for the kinds of research projects that today appear most promising in this field, the Association could exert a further welcome influence.

PART III. THE PROSPECT FOR ACTION

11. *Sources of Support and Leadership*

Readjustments in the structure and operation of the political parties call for a widespread appreciation, by influential parts of the public as well as by political leaders and party officials, of the kinds of change that are needed in order to bring about a more responsible operation of of the two-party system.

1. *The Economic Pressure Groups.* Highly organized special interests with small or no direct voting power are best satisfied if the individual legislator and administrative official are kept defenseless in the face of their special pressure. Organizations with large membership are not in the same category. It is reasonable to expect that those large-membership organizations with wise leadership will generally support the turn toward more responsible parties.

2. *The Party Leaders.* Leaders who represent divergent sectional or other special interests within each party will look with disfavor upon any reforms that hit specifically at their personal vested interests. Most of the forward-looking leaders in each party are convinced that changes should be made.

3. *The Government Officialdom.* Greater program responsibility at the level of the political parties is likely to appeal to administrators and the career officialdom.

4. *Congress.* It cannot be expected that all congressional leaders will be sympathetic to the concept of party responsibility. As leaders of national opinion, influential members of each party in Congress can give strong support to the idea of party responsibility.

5. *The President.* The President can probably be more influential than any other single individual in attaining a better organized majority party, and thus also prompting the minority party to follow suit. With greater party responsibility, the President's position as party leader would correspond in strength to the greater strength of his party.

6. *The Electorate.* The electorate consists of three main groups: (1) those who seldom or never vote; (2) those who vote regularly for the party of their traditional affiliation; and (3) those who base their electoral choice upon the political performance of the two parties, as indicated by the programs they support and the candidates they succeed in putting forward. The rank and file in each party want their party so organized that the views of the party majority will be respected and carried out. It may well be the members of the third group who, in making their choices at election time, will decide the question of our country's progress in the direction of a more responsible party system. It is this group that occupies a place of critical importance in supporting a party system able to shoulder national responsibility.

12. *The Dangers of Inaction*

Four dangers warrant special emphasis. The first danger is that the inadequacy of the party system in sustaining well-considered programs

and providing broad public support for them may lead to grave consequences in an explosive era. The second danger is that the American
people may go too far for the safety of constitutional government in
compensating for this inadequacy by shifting excessive responsibility to
the President. The third danger is that with growing public cynicism
and continuing proof of the ineffectiveness of the party system the nation
may eventually witness the disintegration of the two major parties.
The fourth danger is that the incapacity of the two parties for consistent
action based on meaningful programs may rally support for extremist
parties poles apart, each fanatically bent on imposing on the country
its particular panacea.

1. *The Danger of an Explosive Era.* The political foundation of appropriate governmental programs is very unstable when it is not supplied
by responsible party action.

2. *The Danger of Overextending the Presidency.* Dependable political
support has to be built up for the governmental program. When there
is no other place to get that done, when the political parties fail to do
it, it is tempting to turn to the President. When the President's program
actually is the sole program, either his party becomes a flock of sheep
or the party falls apart. This concept of the presidency disposes of the
party system by making the President reach directly for the support
of a majority of the voters.

3. *The Danger of Disintegration of the Two Parties.* A chance that the
electorate will turn its back upon the two parties is by no means academic. As a matter of fact, this development has already occurred in
considerable part, and it is still going on. American political institutions
are too firmly grounded upon the two-party system to make its collapse
a small matter.

4. *The Danger of an Unbridgeable Political Cleavage.* If the two parties
do not develop alternative programs that can be executed, the voter's
frustration and the mounting ambiguities of national policy might set
in motion more extreme tendencies to the political left and the political
right. Once a deep political cleavage develops between opposing groups,
each group naturally works to keep it deep. Orientation of the American
two-party system along the lines of meaningful national programs is a
significant step toward avoiding the development of such a cleavage.

PART I. THE NEED FOR GREATER PARTY RESPONSIBILITY

1. *The Role of the Political Parties*

1. *The Parties and Public Policy.* Throughout this report political parties are treated as indispensable instruments of government. That is to say, we proceed on the proposition that *popular government in a nation of more than 150 million people requires political parties which provide the electorate with a proper range of choice between alternatives of action.* The party system thus serves as the main device for bringing into continuing relationship those ideas about liberty, majority rule and leadership which Americans are largely taking for granted.

For the great majority of Americans, the most valuable opportunity to influence the course of public affairs is the choice they are able to make between the parties in the principal elections. While in an election the party alternative necessarily takes the form of a choice between candidates, putting a particular candidate into office is not an end in itself. The concern of the parties with candidates, elections and appointments is misunderstood if it is assumed that parties can afford to bring forth aspirants for office without regard to the views of those so selected. Actually, the party struggle is concerned with the direction of public affairs. Party nominations are no more than a means to this end. In short, party politics inevitably involves public policy in one way or another. *In order to keep the parties apart, one must consider the relations between each and public policy.*

This is not to ignore that in the past the American two-party system has shown little propensity for evolving original or creative ideas about public policy; that it has even been rather sluggish in responding to such ideas in the public interest; that it reflects in an enlarged way those differences throughout the country which are expressed in the operation of the federal structure of government; and that in all political organizations a considerable measure of irrationality manifests itself.

Giving due weight to each of these factors, we are nevertheless led to conclude that the choices provided by the two-party system are valuable to the American people in proportion to their definition in terms of public policy. *The reasons for the growing emphasis on public policy in party politics are to be found, above all, in the very operations of modern government.* With the extraordinary growth of the responsibilities of government, the discussion of public affairs for the most part makes sense only in terms of public policy.

2. *The New Importance of Program.* One of the most pressing require-

15

ments of contemporary politics is for the party in power to furnish a general kind of direction over the government as a whole. *The crux of public affairs lies in the necessity for more effective formulation of general policies and programs and for better integration of all of the far-flung activities of modern government.*

Only large-scale and representative political organizations possess the qualifications needed for these tasks. The ascendancy of national issues in an industrial society, the impact of the widening concern of government with problems of the general welfare, the entrance into the realm of politics of millions of new voters—all of these factors have tended to broaden the base of the parties as the largest political organizations in the country. *It is in terms of party programs that political leaders can attempt to consolidate public attitudes toward the work plans of government.*

Modern public policy, therefore, accentuates the importance of the parties, not as mere brokers between different groups and interests, but as agencies of the electorate. Because it affects unprecedented numbers of people and because it depends for its execution on extensive and widespread public support, modern public policy requires a broad political base. That base can be provided only by the parties, which reach people touched by no other political organization.

3. *The Potentialities of the Party System. The potentialities of the two-party system are suggested, on the one hand, by the fact that for all practical purposes the major parties monopolize elections; and, on the other, by the fact that both parties have in the past managed to adapt themselves to the demands made upon them by external necessities.*

Moreover, in contrast with any other political organization today in existence, the major parties even now are forced to consider public policy at least broadly enough to make it likely for them to win elections. If public esteem of the parties is much less high than it might be, the depressed state of their reputation has resulted in the main from their past indifference to broadly conceived public policy. This indifference has fixed in the popular mind the idea of spoils, patronage and plunder. It is hence not astonishing when one hears a chosen representative assert for the public ear that in his state "people put principles above party." Much of the agitation for nonpartisanship—despite the impossibility of nonpartisan organization on a national level—is rooted in the same attitudes.

Bad reputations die hard, but things are no longer what they used to be. Certainly success in presidential campaigns today is based on broad national appeals to the widest possible constituencies. To a much greater extent than in the past, elections are won by influences and trends that are felt throughout the country. *It is* therefore *good practical politics to reconsider party organization in the light of the changing conditions of politics.*

It appeared desirable in this report to relate the potentialities of the party system to both the conditions that confront the nation and the expected role of the parties. *Happily such an effort entails an application of ideas about the party system that are no longer unfamiliar.*

Consideration of ways and means of producing a more responsible party system leads into the hazards of political invention. This is a challenge that has usually been accepted with misgivings by political scientists, who are trained to describe what is and feel less well qualified to fashion innovations. We hope that our own effort will stimulate both other political scientists and participants in practical politics to attempt similar undertakings on their own account. Only by a continuous process of invention and adjustment can the party system be adapted to meet the needs of our day.

2. *What Kind of Party System Is Needed?*

There is little point to talking about the American party system in terms of its deficiencies and potentialities except against a picture of what the parties ought to be. Our report would be lacking in exactness without an indication of the sort of model we have in mind.

Americans are reasonably well agreed about the purposes served by the two major parties as long as the matter is discussed in generalities. When specific questions are raised, however, agreement is much more limited. We cannot assume, therefore, a commonly shared view about the essential characteristics of the party system. But we can and must state our own view.

In brief, our view is this: *The party system that is needed must be democratic, responsible and effective*—a system that is accountable to the public, respects and expresses differences of opinion, and is able to cope with the great problems of modern government. Some of the implications warrant special statement, which is the purpose of this section.

I. A Stronger Two-party System

1. *The Need for an Effective Party System.* In an era beset with problems of unprecedented magnitude at home and abroad, it is dangerous to drift without a party system that helps the nation to set a general course of policy for the government as a whole. In a two-party system, when both parties are weakened or confused by internal divisions or ineffective organization it is the nation that suffers. When the parties are unable to reach and pursue responsible decisions, difficulties accumulate and cynicism about all democratic institutions grows.

An effective party system requires, first, that the parties are able to bring forth programs to which they commit themselves and, second, that the parties possess sufficient internal cohesion to carry out these programs. In such a system, the party program becomes the work program of the party, so recognized by the party leaders in and out of the government, by the party body as a whole, and by the public. This condition is unattainable unless party institutions have been created through which agreement can be reached about the general position of the party.

Clearly *such a degree of unity within the parties cannot be brought about without party procedures that give a large body of people an opportunity to share in the development of the party program.* One great function of the party system is to bring about the widest possible consent in relation to defined political goals, which provides the majority party with the essential means of building public support for the policies of the government. Democratic procedures in the internal affairs of the parties are best suited to the development of agreement within each party.

2. *The Need for an Effective Opposition Party.* The argument for a stronger party system cannot be divorced from measures designed to make the parties more fully accountable to the public. *The fundamental requirement of such accountability is a two-party system in which the opposition party acts as the critic of the party in power, developing, defining and presenting the policy alternatives which are necessary for a true choice in reaching public decisions.*

Beyond that, the case for the American two-party system need not be restated here. The two-party system is so strongly rooted in the political traditions of this country and public preference for it is so well established that consideration of other possibilities seems entirely academic. When we speak of the parties without further qualification, we mean throughout our report the two major parties. The inference is not that we consider third or minor parties undesirable or ineffectual within their limited orbit. Rather, we feel that the minor parties in the longer run have failed to leave a lasting imprint upon both the two-party system and the basic processes of American government.

In spite of the fact that the two-party system is part of the American political tradition, it cannot be said that the role of the opposition party is well understood. This is unfortunate because democratic government is greatly influenced by the character of the opposition party. The measures proposed elsewhere in our report to help the party in power to clarify its policies are equally applicable to the opposition.

The opposition most conducive to responsible government is an organized party opposition, produced by the organic operation of the two-party system. When there are two parties identifiable by the kinds of action they propose, the voters have an actual choice. On the other hand, the sort of opposition presented by a coalition that cuts across party lines, as a regular thing, tends to deprive the public of a meaningful alternative. When such coalitions are formed after the elections are over, the public usually finds it difficult to understand the new situation and to reconcile it with the purpose of the ballot. Moreover, on that basis it is next to impossible to hold either party responsible for its political record. This is a serious source of public discontent.

II. Better Integrated Parties

1. *The Need for a Party System with Greater Resistance to Pressure.* As a consciously defined and consistently followed line of action keeps individuals from losing themselves in irresponsible ventures, so a program-conscious party develops greater resistance against the inroads of pressure groups.

The value of special-interest groups in a diversified society made up of countless groupings and specializations should be obvious. But organized interest groups cannot do the job of the parties. Indeed, it is only when a working formula of the public interest in its *general* character is made manifest by the parties in terms of coherent programs that the claims of interest groups can be adjusted on the basis of political responsibility. Such adjustment, once again, calls for the party's ability to honor its word.

There is little to suggest that the phenomenal growth of interest organizations in recent decades has come to its end. Organization along such lines is a characteristic feature of our civilization. To some extent these interest groups have replaced or absorbed into themselves older local institutions in that they make it possible for the government and substantial segments of the nation to maintain contact with each other. It must be obvious, however, that *the whole development makes necessary a reinforced party system that can cope with the multiplied organized pressures.* The alternative would be a scheme perhaps best described as government by pressure groups intent upon using the parties to deflect political attention from themselves.

By themselves, the interest groups cannot attempt to define public policy democratically. Coherent public policies do not emerge as the mathematical result of the claims of all of the pressure groups. The integration of the interest groups into the political system is a function of the parties. Any tendency in the direction of a strengthened party system encourages the interest groups to align themselves with one or the other of the major parties. Such a tendency is already at work. One of the noteworthy features of contemporary American politics is the fact that not a few interest groups have found it impossible to remain neutral toward both parties. To illustrate, the entry of organized labor upon the political scene has in turn impelled antagonistic special interests to coalesce in closer political alignments.

In one respect the growth of the modern interest groups is exerting a direct effect upon the internal distribution of power within the parties. They counteract and offset local interests; they are a nationalizing influence. Indeed, the proliferation of interest groups has been one of the factors in the rise of national issues because these groups tend to organize and define their objectives on a national scale.

Parties whose political commitments count are of particular significance to interest organizations with large membership such as exist among industrial workers and farmers, but to a lesser extent also among businessmen. Unlike the great majority of pressure groups, these organizations through their membership—and in proportion to their voting strength—are able to play a measurable role in elections. Interest groups of this kind are the equivalent of organizations of voters. For reasons of mutual interest, the relationship between them and the parties tends to become explicit and continuing.

A stronger party system is less likely to give cause for the deterioration and confusion of purposes which sometimes passes for compromise but is really an unjustifiable surrender to narrow interests. *Compromise among interests is compatible with the aims of a free society only when the terms of reference reflect an openly acknowledged concept of the public interest.* There is every reason to insist that the parties be held accountable to the public for the compromises they accept.

2. *The Need for a Party System with Sufficient Party Loyalty.* It is here not suggested, of course, that the parties should disagree about everything. Parties do not, and need not, take a position on all questions that allow for controversy. The proper function of the parties is to develop and define policy alternatives on matters likely to be of interest to the whole country, on issues related to the responsibility of the parties for the conduct of either the government or the opposition.

Needed clarification of party policy in itself *will not cause the parties to differ more fundamentally or more sharply than they have in the past.* The contrary is much more likely to be the case. The clarification of party policy may be expected to produce a more reasonable discussion of public affairs, more closely related to the political performance of the parties in their actions rather than their words. *Nor is it to be assumed that increasing concern with their programs will cause the parties to erect between themselves an ideological wall.* There is no real ideological division in the American electorate, and hence programs of action presented by responsible parties for the voter's support could hardly be expected to reflect or strive toward such division.

It is true at the same time that ultimately any political party must establish some conditions for membership and place some obligations on its representatives in government. Without so defining its identity the party is in danger of ceasing to be a party. To make party policy effective the *parties have the right and the duty to announce the terms to govern participation in the common enterprise.* This basic proposition is rarely denied, nor are precedents lacking. But there are practical difficulties in the way of applying restraints upon those who disregard the stated terms.

It is obvious that an effective party cannot be based merely or primarily on the expulsion of the disloyal. To impose discipline in any voluntary association is possible only as a last resort and only when a wide consensus is present within the association. Discipline and consensus are simply the front and rear sides of the same coin. *The emphasis in all consideration of party discipline must be,* therefore, *on positive measures to create a strong and general agreement on policies.* Thereafter, the problem of discipline is secondary and marginal.

When the membership of the party has become well aware of party policy and stands behind it, assumptions about teamwork within the party are likely to pervade the whole organization. Ultimately it is the electorate itself which will determine how firmly it wants the lines of party allegiance to be drawn. Yet even a small shift of emphasis toward party cohesion is likely to produce changes not only in the structure of the parties but also in the degree to which members identify themselves with their party.

Party unity is always a relative matter. It may be fostered, but the whole weight of tradition in American politics is against very rigid party discipline. As a general rule, the parties have a basis for expecting adherence to the party program when their position is reasonably explicit. Thus it is evident that the disciplinary difficulties of the parties do not result primarily from a reluctance to impose restraints but from the neglect of positive measures to give meaning to party programs.

As for party cohesion in Congress, the parties have done little to build up the kind of unity within the congressional party that is now so widely desired. Traditionally congressional candidates are treated as if they were the orphans of the political system, with no truly adequate party mechanism available for the conduct of their campaigns. Enjoying remarkably little national or local party support, congressional candidates have mostly been left to cope with the political hazards of their occupation on their own account. *A basis for party cohesion in Congress will be established as soon as the parties interest themselves sufficiently in their congressional candidates to set up strong and active campaign organizations in the constituencies.* Discipline is less a matter of what the parties do *to* their congressional candidates than what the parties do *for* them.

III. More Responsible Parties

1. *The Need for Parties Responsible to the Public. Party responsibility means the responsibility of both parties to the general public, as enforced in elections.*

Responsibility of the party in power centers on the conduct of the government, usually in terms of policies. The party in power has a responsibility, broadly defined, for the general management of the government, for its manner of getting results, for the results achieved, for the consequences of inaction as well as action, for the intended and unintended outcome of its conduct of public affairs, for all that it plans to do, for all that it might have foreseen, for the leadership it provides, for the acts of all of its agents, and for what it says as well as for what it does.

Party responsibility includes the responsibility of the opposition party, also broadly defined, for the conduct of its opposition, for the management of public discussion, for the development of alternative policies and programs, for the bipartisan policies which it supports, for its failures and successes in developing the issues of public policy, and for its leadership of public opinion. The opposition is as responsible for its record in Congress as is the party in power. It is important that the opposition party be effective but it is equally important that it be responsible, for an irresponsible opposition is dangerous to the whole political system.

Party responsibility to the public, enforced in elections, implies that there be more than one party, for the public can hold a party responsible only if it has a choice. Again, unless the parties identify themselves with programs, the public is unable to make an intelligent choice between them. The public can understand the general management of the government only in terms of policies. When the parties lack the capacity to define their actions in terms of policies, they turn irresponsible because the electoral choice between the parties becomes devoid of meaning.

As a means of achieving responsibility, the clarification of party policy also tends to keep public debate on a more realistic level, restraining the inclination of party spokesmen to make unsubstantiated statements and charges. When party policy is made clear, the result to be expected is a more reasonable and profitable discussion, tied more closely to the record of party action. When there is no clear basis for rating party performance, when party policies cannot be defined in terms of a concrete program, party debate tears itself loose from the facts. Then wild fictions are used to excite the imagination of the public.

2. *The Need for Parties Responsible to Their Members. Party responsibility includes also the responsibility of party leaders to the party membership, as enforced in primaries, caucuses and conventions.* To this end the internal processes of the parties must be democratic, the party members must have an opportunity to participate in intraparty business, and the leaders must be accountable to the party. Responsibility demands that the parties concern themselves with the development of good relations between the leaders and the members. Only thus can the parties act as intermediaries between the government and the people. Strengthening the parties involves, therefore, the improvement of the internal democratic processes by which the leaders of the party are kept in contact with the members.

The external and the internal kinds of party responsibility need not conflict. Responsibility of party leaders to party members promotes the clarification of party policy when it means that the leaders find it necessary to explain the policy to the membership. Certainly the lack of unity within the membership cannot be overcome by the fiat of an irresponsible party leadership. A democratic internal procedure can be used not merely to test the strength of the various factions within a party but also to resolve the conflicts. The motives for enlarging the areas of agreement within the parties are persuasive because unity is the condition of success.

Intraparty conflict will be minimized if it is generally recognized that national, state and local party leaders have a common responsibility to the party membership. Intraparty conflict is invited and exaggerated by dogmas that assign to local party leaders an exclusive right to appeal to the party membership in their area.

Occasions may arise in which the parties will find it necessary to apply sanctions against a state or local party organization, especially when that organization is in open rebellion against policies established for the whole party. There are a variety of ways in which recognition may be withdrawn. It is possible to refuse to seat delegates to the National Convention; to drop from the National Committee members representing the dissident state organization; to deny legislative committee assignments to members of Congress sponsored by the disloyal organization; and to appeal directly to the party membership in the state or locality, perhaps even promoting a rival organization. The power to take strong measures is there.

It would be unfortunate, however, if the problem of party unity were thought of as primarily a matter of punishment. Nothing prevents the parties from explaining themselves to their own members. The party members have power to insist that local and state party organizations and leaders cooperate with the party as a whole; all the members need is a better opportunity to find out what party politics is about. The need for sanctions is relatively small when state and local organizations are not treated as the restricted preserve of their immediate leaders. National party leaders ought to have access to party members everywhere as a normal and regular procedure because they share with local party leaders responsibility to the same party membership. It would always be proper for the national party leaders to discuss all party matters with the membership of any state or local party organization. Considering their great prestige, wise and able national party leaders will need very little more than this opportunity.

The political developments of our time place a heavy emphasis on national issues as the basis of party programs. As a result, the party membership is coming to look to the national party leaders for a larger role in intraparty affairs. There is some evidence of growing general agreement within the membership of each party, strong enough to form a basis of party unity, provided the parties maintain close contact with their own supporters.

In particular, *national party leaders have a legitimate interest in the nomination of congressional candidates,* though normally they try hard to avoid the appearance of any intervention. Depending on the circumstances, this interest can be expressed quite sufficiently by seeking a chance to discuss the nomination with the party membership in the congressional district. On the other hand, it should not be assumed that state and local party leaders usually have an interest in congressional nominations antagonistic to the interest of the national leaders in maintaining the general party policy. As a matter of fact, congressional nominations are not considered great prizes by the local party organization as generally as one might think. It is neglect of congressional nominations and elections more than any other factor that weakens party unity in Congress. It should be added, however, that what is said here about intraparty relations with respect to congressional nominations applies also to other party nominations.

3. *The Inadequacy of the Existing Party System*

The existing party system is inadequately prepared to meet the demands now being made upon it chiefly because its central institutions are not well organized to deal with national questions. The sort of party organization needed today is indirectly suggested by the origin of the traditional party structure. This structure developed in a period in which local interests were dominant and positive governmental action at the national level did not play the role it assumed later.

I. Beginning Transition

1. *Change and Self-examination.* Having outlined the kind of party system we accept as our basic model, we are now able to list briefly some of the principal deficiencies of the existing national party institutions. At the same time we can identify some of the conspicuous failings that show up in the operations of the two parties, in particular their failure to bring about adequate popular participation in politics and to develop satisfactory relations between the central and the local party organizations.

Marked changes have occurred *in the structure and processes of American society* during the twentieth century. Their general effect upon the political scene will be indicated in the following section. Here it will be enough to point out that most of these changes *have necessarily affected the party system.* In many respects the party system is today far from what it was fifty years ago, even though there has not been as yet a conscious and planned adjustment. When a party system is undergoing such a slow transformation, it is difficult to describe its operation accurately or to enumerate its deficiencies precisely as they now exist. The Democratic party is today almost a new creation, produced since 1932. Some of its leaders have given much thought to its present-day characteristics. On the opposite side, the Republican party has been the subject of extensive and repeated self-examination for nearly two decades. It is *the prevailing climate of self-examination as well as the current tendencies toward change in the party system* that *give point to inquiries like that represented by our report.*

2. *Burden of the Past.* Despite these tendencies toward change, however, *formal party organization in its main features is still substantially what it was before the Civil War.* Aside from the adoption of the direct primary, organizational forms have not been overhauled for nearly a century. The result is that the parties are now probably the most archaic institutions in the United States.

Under these circumstances, it is not surprising that *the main trends of American politics,* especially the emphasis on effective national action, *have tended to outflank the party system.* Until rather recently neither of the two parties has found it necessary to concern itself seriously with the question of adequate party organization at the national level. The familiar description of the parties as loose confederations of state and local machines has too long remained reasonably accurate.

II. Some Basic Problems

Party institutions and their operations cannot be divorced from the general conditions that govern the nature of the party system. Before we focus specifically on the deficiencies of existing party institutions, we must account for some of the more important factors that impress themselves upon both major parties.

What are the general features of party organization that have cast up continuing problems?

1. *The Federal Basis. The two parties are organized on a federal basis,* probably as a natural result of our federal type of government. In Charles E. Merriam's words, "The American party system has its roots in the states. Its regulation and control is conducted almost wholly, although not entirely, by the states acting separately."[1] This means that *the national and state party organizations are largely independent of one another,* each operating within its own sphere, *without appreciable common approach to problems of party policy and strategy.*

Such independence has led to frequent and sharp differences between state and national organizations. Antagonisms are illustrated by such terms as national Republicans and Wisconsin Republicans, national Democrats and Dixiecrats. Moreover, state party organizations too often define their interests quite narrowly. This does not merely mean substantial disregard of national needs or matters of national interest, but it also means piecemeal as well as one-sided use of state power and state resources. As John M. Gaus has put it, "In many states—probably in almost all—the party systems are inadequate as instruments for reflecting the needs of our citizens for carefully thought-out, alternative programs of public housekeeping."[2]

It is not being argued here that the party system should be cut free from its federal basis. Federalism is not a negative influence in itself; it is equally capable of positive accomplishments in the public interest. Whether it works in the one or the other direction depends in large part on how well the balance of forces within a federal organization accords with the needs of society. In the case of the American party system, *the real issue is not over the federal form of organization but over the right balance of forces within this type of organization.*

On that score, the party system is weighted much more heavily toward the state-local side than is true today of the federal system of government in the United States. The gap produces serious disabilities in government. It needs to be closed, even though obviously our traditions

---

[1] Charles E. Merriam, "State Government at Mid-Century," *State Government,* Vol. 23, p. 118 (June, 1950).

[2] John M. Gaus, "The States Are in the Middle," *ibid.,* p. 140.

of localism, states rights and sectionalism will inevitably affect the pace of progress that can be expected.

A corollary of the kind of federalism now expressed in the party system is an excessive measure of internal separatism. The congressional party organization is independent of the national organization, and the House and Senate organizations of the same party are independent of each other. As a result, cooperation between these parts of the national party structure has not been easy to secure.

2. *The Location of Leadership.* In part because of the centrifugal drives that run through the party system, *party organization does not vest leadership of the party as a whole in either a single person or a committee.* The President, by virtue of his conspicuous position and his real as well as symbolic role in public opinion, is commonly considered the leader of his party. If he has a vigorous personality and the disposition to press his views on party policy and strategy, he may become the actual leader during his presidential term. But even the President has no official position within the party organization, and his leadership is often resented and opposed. The presidential nominee of the defeated party is generally recognized as the "titular leader" of his party, yet the very title implies a lack of authority.

The National Chairman is most nearly in the top position, but if he tries to exercise initiative and leadership in matters other than the presidential campaign, his authority is almost certain to be challenged. Ill feeling, rather than harmony of policy and action, is likely to result. In sum, *there is at present no central figure or organ which could claim authority to take up party problems, policies and strategy.*

3. *The Ambiguity of Membership.* The vagueness of formal leadership that prevails at the top has its counterpart in the vagueness of formal membership at the bottom. *No understandings or rules or criteria exist with respect to membership in a party.* The general situation was well put by Senator Borah in a statement made in 1923:

Any man who can carry a Republican primary is a Republican. He might believe in free trade, in unconditional membership in the League of Nations, in states' rights, and in every policy that the Democratic party ever advocated; yet, if he carried his Republican primary, he would be a Republican. He might go to the other extreme and believe in the communistic state, in the dictatorship of the proletariat, in the abolition of private property, and in the extermination of the bourgeoisie; yet, if he carried his Republican primary, he would still be a Republican.

It is obviously difficult, if not impossible, to secure anything like harmony of policy and action within political parties so loosely organized as this. On the other hand, it is easy to see that the voter's political choice when confined to candidates without a common bond in terms of program amounts to no more than taking a chance with an individual candidate. *Those who suggest that elections should deal with personalities but not with programs suggest at the same time that party membership should mean nothing at all.*

III. Specific Deficiencies

So much for the most conspicuous consequences that stem from the general features of existing party organization. Now let us consider some more specific aspects pertinent to a reorganization of the national party structure.

1. *National Party Organs. The National Convention, as at present constituted and operated, is an unwieldy, unrepresentative and less than responsible body.* In 1948 the Republican convention was composed of 1,094 delegates, and the Democratic convention of 1,234, with an equal additional number of alternates in each case. Both conventions are expected to be still larger in 1952.

The unrepresentative character of the convention has been recognized in both parties by changes in the apportionment of delegates. Yet no one would maintain in either case that the party's rank-and-file strength in the several states is truly represented. The apportionment of delegates to the Democratic National Convention is based, not on the number of Democratic voters in the various states, but on the apportionment of presidential electors. Theoretically, therefore, the delegates represent simply population—Republican voters and nonvoters as well as Democratic voters. Because the rural population is greatly overrepresented in Congress, the urban centers, though virtually the party's backbone, are strongly discriminated against. The following table illustrates the extent of this distortion in eleven states.

Democratic National Convention, 1948

State	Democratic voters per delegate
Maine	11,191
Vermont	7,443
Connecticut	21,164
New York	28,960
Pennsylvania	26,955
Illinois	33,245
Wyoming	8,725
Nevada	3,129
Texas	15,014
South Carolina	1,721
Louisiana	5,680

In spite of a number of attempts to reduce the overrepresentation of southern Republicans in the Republican National Convention it is clear from the next table that much remains to be done.

Republican National Convention, 1948

State	Republican voters per delegate
New York	29,290
Pennsylvania	19,021
Ohio	27,277
Kansas	24,884
South Carolina	894
Georgia	5,478
Alabama	2,923
Mississippi	630
Louisiana	5,589

This lack of balance in representation, together with the peculiar atmosphere within which the Convention operates, makes it very hard for such a body to act in a deliberative and responsible manner. The moral authority of the National Convention to act in the name of the whole party would be greatly strengthened if more care were used to make the convention really representative of the party as a whole.

It can be said equally well of other institutions at the national level that they are not very well suited to carry today's burdens of an effective party system. *The National Committee is seldom a generally influential body and much less a working body.* Indeed, it rarely meets at all.

In *House and Senate*, the *campaign* committee of each party is concerned with aiding in the reelection of members of its chamber. These *committees do not always have a good working relationship with the National Committee.* They do not plan joint election strategy for both chambers and traditionally accept little responsibility for party leadership. Only in the past generation have the parties shown signs of developing a continuous working organization at the national level. *Although their interest in questions of party policy has grown, the national party organs are not so constituted nor so coordinated as to make it simple for them to pay enough attention to these questions.*

2. *Party Platforms.* The growing importance of national issues in American politics puts weight into the formulation of general statements of party policy. Of course, no single statement of party policy can express the whole program of the party in all of its particulars, including questions of timing. But it is obvious that a serious attempt to define the propositions on which the parties intend to seek the voter's support would serve both party unity and party responsibility.

One of the reasons for the widespread lack of respect for party platforms is that they have seldom been used by the parties to get a mandate from the people. By and large, *alternatives between the parties are defined so badly that it is often difficult to determine what the election has decided even in broadest terms.* Yet unused resources are available to the parties in the democratic process itself if they learn to use a statement of policy as the basis for the election campaign. Platforms acquire authority when they are so used.

The prevailing procedure for the writing and adoption of national party platforms is too hurried and too remote from the process by which actual decisions are made to command the respect of the whole party and the electorate. The drafting of a platform ought to be the work of months, not of a day or two; it ought to be linked closely with the formulation of party policy as a continuing activity. Party policy—in its bricks and straws— is made, applied, explored and tested in congressional and presidential decisions, in the executive departments, in the work of research staffs, in committee hearings, and in congressional debates. No party convention can pull a party program out of the air. *The platform should be the end product of a long search for a working agreement within the party.*

3. *Intraparty Democracy.* One of the principal functions of the parties —in terms of the concept of party we elaborated in the preceding section—is to extend to the fullest the citizen's participation in public affairs. Measured by this standard, the existing parties are painfully deficient. Direct primary legislation offers opportunities for the creation of a broad base on which to build the party structure, but these opportunities have rarely been fully utilized.

Too little consideration has been given to ways and means of bringing about a constructive relationship between the party and its members. Indeed, any organization really concerned about this relationship does a multitude of things that American parties generally do not do to maintain close contact with the membership. Party membership ought to become a year-round matter, both with constructive activities by the members and with mechanisms by which the party organizations can absorb the benefits of wider political participation.

If we take the total vote cast in elections as a crude measure of the effectiveness of the parties *in making the most of popular participation, the performance of American parties is very unsatisfactory.* In the 1948 presidential election, approximately 47,000,000 citizens of voting age did not vote. In the congressional election of 1946 only a little more than one-third of the potential vote was cast. This is evidence of low-grade performance, compared with the record of the parties in other democratic countries.

4. *Party Research.* An unimaginative attitude is shown by party organizations in their reluctance to develop party research to the full level of its potentialities. In view of the complexity and difficulty of the problems with which the parties must deal, it can hardly be denied that *a party stands as much in need of research as does business enterprise or the government itself.*

It is a remarkable indication of small party interest, for instance, that politically useful research by government agencies is being carried on to a very limited extent. Thus the United States Census Bureau does not collect and publish comprehensive election statistics, and much of the raw statistical data for party research is not produced by government. Relatively little use has been made by the parties of social survey techniques as a basis for political campaigns. Nor have the parties shown much interest in the study of the social, economic and psychological factors that influence the results of the election contests. At a time when the discussion of public policy is necessarily becoming the focus of party business, the parties have not yet established research staffs adequately equipped to provide party leaders with technical data and findings grounded in scientific analysis.

4. *New Demands Upon Party Leadership*

I. The Nature of Modern Public Policy

1. *Broad Range of Policy. The expanding responsibilities of modern government have brought about so extensive an interlacing of governmental action with the country's economic and social life that the need for coordinated and coherent programs, legislative as well as administrative, has become paramount.* Formulating and executing such general programs involves more than technical knowledge. *In a democracy no general program can be adopted and carried out without wide political support.* Support must be strong enough and stable enough to guard the program as far as possible against such drives as come forth constantly from a multitude of special interests seeking their own ends. This kind of political support can be mobilized on a continuing basis only by stronger parties.

Broad governmental programs need to be built on a foundation of political commitments as written into the programs of adequately organized parties. This is true today also of governmental programs erected on bipartisan backing. In that respect the political requirements to sustain American diplomacy are very different from those of the period before World War I, for example. As Walter Lippmann has recently written of the requirements of bipartisan foreign policy, "It takes two organized parties, each with its recognized leaders in the field of foreign affairs. Today neither party is organized. Neither party has leaders in the field of foreign affairs. In this chaos no Secretary of State can function successfully."[1]

2. *Impact on the Public.* What is said here about the need for an adequate political base for foreign policy applies equally to such other large sectors of public concern as national defense and economic policy. In each area, the problems are so interrelated that the activities of the government must be integrated over a very wide front. *In a predominantly industrial society, public policy tends to be widely inclusive, involving in its objectives and effects very large segments of the public or even the whole country.*

This is true of a great many fields, such as labor relations, credit regulation, social security, housing, price support, aid to veterans, and even revenue administration. To quote the Bureau of Internal Revenue, ". . . the Bureau . . . reaches into every town and hamlet throughout the United States and directly affects the finances of some 65 million people in the form of one or more levies."[2] Mark Sullivan has described the activities of the United States Department of Agriculture in language strikingly similar, if with a bit of poetic license: "It enters every home in the country, stands beside every citizen as he eats his meals, and every member of his family. It determines or conclusively influences the price of nearly every form of food. In doing this the department goes a second time into the homes of a large class of citizens, the farmers. To them it in many cases pays large amounts of money to buy large quantities of their crops and keep them off the market, in order to support the price."[3]

3. *Governmental Program Machinery. On the side of government, in the administrative and the legislative spheres, the twin needs for program formulation and for program machinery have long been recognized.* A series of laws has aimed in this direction. The Budget and Accounting Act of 1921, with its emphasis on the government's financial program and thus on the government's work plan in its entirety, including the legislative program of the President; the Employment Act of 1946, in its concern with a program to sustain high-level production and employment; the Legislative Reorganization Act of the same year, giving added strength to Congress in the exercise of its function of review of programs proposed by the executive branch; the National Security Act of 1947,

---

[1] *New York Herald Tribune,* March 27, 1950.
[2] *The Budget for the Fiscal Year 1951,* p. 1033.
[3] *New York Herald Tribune,* March 24, 1950.

creating the National Security Council as policy coordinator for national defense—these acts illustrate the trend.

The governmental advance toward program formulation needs now to be paralleled in the political sphere proper—above all in the party system. Without mobilization of political support the best-conceived programs of modern government come to naught.

II. Rise of Nation-wide Policy Issues

1. *An Historic Trend.* Even if the international scene did not look as it does, *the changes in the nature and scope of public policy* here indicated would press upon the political process. For they *are the result of changes in the social structure and the economy of the United States.* The long-range transformations expressed in industrialization and urbanization and the revolution in transportation and communication were bound to create a truly national economy and to affect significantly the bases of American politics.

After the experience of the great depression in the thirties, the public has become particularly conscious of the need for economic stability. It is now regarded as obvious by large groups of voters that only the national government has the span of jurisdiction and resources adequate to cope with this problem. On the same grounds many of the other anxieties which people feel living in the uncertain conditions of the modern world stimulate demands on the national government.

2. *Past and Present Factors.* It is much the same thing to say that *there has been in recent decades a continuing decline of sectionalism,* first noted by Arthur N. Holcombe nearly twenty years ago. Statistical evidence such as is available for the last generation shows that the most significant political trends in the country have been national, not sectional or local. This is not to say that sectionalism is likely to drop to insignificance as a factor in American politics. Here as elsewhere in the political system, change is a matter of degree. The relative decline of the strength of sectional alignments is nevertheless a matter of great consequence. Elections are increasingly won and lost by influences felt throughout the land.

The measurable shift from sectional to national politics cannot fail to have a corresponding effect on party organization and the locus of power within the parties. *Party organization designed to deal with the increasing volume of national issues must give wider range to the national party leadership.* With sectionalism in steady if slow decline, a change of the rules of politics is taking place. Long-range political success is likely to come to those leaders and that party quickest to go by the new rules.

As long as sectional alignments were dominant in American politics, strong party organization was not needed. As a matter of fact, sectionalism has long been the great enemy of true party organization. In its extreme form, sectionalism tends to eliminate the opposition party altogether. In the one-party areas so often linked to sectional alignments, the opposition party is a mere shadow.

Without effective party opposition, strong organization becomes very difficult to attain even for the dominant party. Illustrative of this condition has been the Solid South, where as a rule neither of the parties has produced strong state and local organizations, but only rather informal groupings built around individual leaders.

On the other hand, a stronger national party organization tends to play down sectional differences. The transition from predominantly sectional to primarily national politics generates a trend toward appropriate reorganization of the parties. It is in the main this trend that forms the practical base for the revision of party structure and procedures contemplated in our report.

3. *New Interest Groups in Politics. The economic and social factors that have reduced the weight of sectionalism have also resulted in the development of a new type of interest groups, built upon large membership.* These new interest groups, found principally in the areas of industrial labor and agriculture, are pursuing a novel political strategy. *To a much greater extent than in the past, they operate as if they were auxiliary organizations of one or the other party.* The growing conversion of most of the labor movement to party action is a case in point. Labor organizations now participate energetically in election contests. They register voters, take part in the nominating process, raise campaign funds, issue campaign literature and perform other functions once on the whole reserved for the parties.

Thus the old local monopolies of the regular party organizations have been broken by new large-membership groups. To a very considerable extent the regular party organizations are now so yoked into a partnership with the newcomers that they have lost much of their old freedom of action. The successful political leader in the future is likely to be one who is skillful in maintaining a good working alliance between the older and the newer types of political organization. This applies partly even to conditions today.

The emphasis of the new large-membership organizations is on national rather than sectional issues. What is no less significant, the interests of the membership are not identified with any single product or commodity. Farmers, for instance, cannot hope to prosper in an ailing economy. Workers must measure their pay against the level of prices as well as the value of social security. Hence the large-membership groups are inevitably pushed into consideration of all of the factors that affect the national well-being. How parties stand on programs designed to bring about stability and healthy expansion in the economy as a whole is therefore of great concern to most of the new groups in American politics.

5. *The Question of Constitutional Amendment*

1. *A Cabinet System?* It is altogether clear that party responsibility cannot be legislated into being. Not a few Americans have argued, however, that something like the British system of responsible cabinet government would have to be grafted to ours before an effective party system could come about in the United States. Usually this idea takes the form of proposals to amend the Constitution to give the President the right to dissolve Congress and to call a new election at any time, besides certain other changes in the Constitution.

A responsible cabinet system makes the leaders of the majority party in the legislature the heads of the executive departments, *collectively accountable* to their own legislative majority *for the conduct of the government.* Such a relationship prompts close cooperation between the executive and legislative branches. The legislative majority of the cabinet forms a party team which as such can readily be held responsible for its policies. This governmental system is built around the parties, which play the key role in it.

2. *Strong Parties as a Condition.* We do not here need to take a position on the abstract merits of the cabinet system. On the question whether it could be successfully fitted into the American scheme of congressional-presidential government, opinions are widely divided. Even if it were conceded to be desirable *to amend the Constitution in order to create a responsible cabinet system,* it should be plain that this *is not a practicable way of getting more effective parties.* Such an amendment, if it offered likelihood of being adopted at all, would make sense only when the parties have actually demonstrated the strength they now lack. When they show that strength, a constitutional amendment to achieve this end would be unnecessary.

On the other hand, the experience of foreign countries suggests that adoption of the cabinet system does not automatically result in an effective party system. Cabinet systems differ in their results and affect the party system in different ways. Moreover, it is easy to overestimate not only the expected benefits of a constitutional amendment but also the rigidity of the existing constitutional arrangements in the United States. Certainly the roles of the President and Congress are defined by the Constitution in terms that leave both free to cooperate and to rely on the concept of party responsibility.

3. *Adaptation within the Constitution. The parties can do much to adapt the usages under the Constitution to their purposes.* When strong enough, the parties obviously can furnish the President and Congress a political basis of cooperation within the Constitution as it stands today.

Actually the parties have not carefully explored the opportunities they have for more responsible operation under existing constitutional arrangements. It is logical first to find out what can be done under present conditions to invigorate the parties before accepting the conclusion that action has to begin with changing a constitutional system that did not contemplate the growing need for party responsibility when it was set up.

PART II. PROPOSALS FOR PARTY RESPONSIBILITY

6. *National Party Organization*

We have summarized the main problems that arise in the present-day operation of the American two-party system. We now turn to an indication of the direction in which remedies might be sought. This is best done by setting forth specific proposals for creating a more suitable national party structure.

Each of these proposals allows for modifications in detail. We do not intend to be sticklers for particulars. Our proposals are meant to suggest a general line of approach. We shall not try to be exhaustive in elaborating upon each proposal.

I. Principal Party Bodies

1. *The National Convention.* It has already been said earlier that the National Convention is unwieldy, unrepresentative and less than responsible in mandate and action. The abuse resulting from an undemocratic system of representation was, in fact, recognized by many Republicans almost from the beginning of the Republican party, and has been corrected for that party to a considerable extent. The Democratic party also recognized the need for improvement at the Convention in 1936, and a new rule of apportionment became effective in 1944.[1] But in either case the existing formula falls distinctly short of true representation of the party's grassroots strength in the individual states.

To allow the convention to act in a responsible manner, President Wilson proposed to Congress in his first annual message in 1913 a drastic change in the convention system. He recommended a national presidential primary and retention of the convention only for the purpose of declaring the results of the primary and formulating the party platform. Even for these purposes the convention was to be no longer a delegate convention, but an ex-officio convention of approximately 600 members, made up of the presidential nominees, the congressional nominees, the party's hold-over members of the Senate, and the members of the National Committee. As Wilson conceived it, the convention

---

[1] The present Republican apportionment rule is to allot two delegates at large for each Senator and each Representative at large to represent the state as such (which, to this extent, is based on the Electoral College principle); six additional delegates to each state that went Republican for President or Senator at the preceding elections; and otherwise representation based upon party strength in the congressional districts. The Democratic rule maintains the system of representation based upon the Electoral College, but adds a bonus of four delegates to states that went Democratic at the preceding presidential election.

37

would be made up of those who are responsible for the management of the party and for the determination and execution of the party policies.

As a practical matter the National Convention, in spite of its short-comings, has become one of the traditional party agencies. *We assume its continuation as the principal representative and deliberative organ of the party.* With certain modifications, the convention can quite satis-factorily attend to its customary functions. These are to nominate presidential candidates (or, should the presidential primary be estab-lished on a national scale, to declare the results); to adopt or approve the party platform; to adopt rules and regulations governing the party; and in general to act as the supreme organ of the party.

But in the interest of greater effectiveness *the convention should meet at least biennially* instead of only quadrennially as at present, *with easy provision for special meetings. It also should cease to be a delegate conven-tion of unwieldy size.* Much better results could be attained with a con-vention of not more than 500–600 members, composed mostly of dele-gates elected directly by the party voters on a more representative basis (300–350 members), a substantial number of ex-officio members (the National Committee, state party chairmen, congressional leaders— probably about 150 altogether), and a selected group of prominent party leaders outside the party organizations (probably 25).

This proposal, which is a modification of President Wilson's, would achieve several things. It would provide a convention representative of the party voters and of the party organization, national and state. It would afford opportunity for expressing and harmonizing the views and interests of the different elements in the party. It would be small enough to make possible deliberation and action on program matters. And it would promote a more responsible consideration of the various problems before the party.

Such a convention should not only meet more frequently, but should also hold longer sessions, in order that it may actually deliberate upon and transact the business that properly comes before the highest repre-sentative assembly of the party.

2. *The National Committee.* The National Committee is another tra-ditional party agency, primarily concerned with the success of the presidential campaign. Although it is nominally chosen by the National Convention and the agent of that body, state legislation and party practice have modified this concept. Both have introduced various methods of selection (by state committee, by state convention, by the party voters at the primary, by the delegations to the National Conven-tion) which have in substance, if not in form, replaced selection by the National Convention.

As a result, the National Committee has become independent of the convention rather than being subordinate to it. The individual members of the National Committee are encouraged to think of themselves as state rather than national party officials. National party authority has thus been weakened.

In view of the state legislation on the subject, it may seem futile to urge uniformity of selection. But *it is highly desirable for the National Convention to reassert its authority over the National Committee through a more active participation in the final selection of the committee membership.* This is still the convention's right under the party rules and practices. In this way, control could be exercised so that only those would be chosen for the National Committee who could be counted on to support the policies and candidates agreed upon by the convention.

In contrast with the present mathematical state equality, *it is also desirable that the members of the National Committee reflect the actual strength of the party within the areas they represent.* For this purpose the principle of unit representation should be applied. This principle is widely used in the operations of state and local party committees. In Illinois, for example, the respective members of the state, county and municipal party committees cast a vote equal to the total party vote in the areas they represent.

Applied to the National Committee, each of the two members from a state might be given a vote equal in weight to one-half of the party vote in that state, or on some other proportionate basis. This would be much more equitable than the individual and equal vote now cast by members of the National Committee, which gives the New York members no more weight than the Nevada or Georgia members. It would also serve as an inducement to strengthen the party and bring out the vote in each area. Finally, it would produce a stronger sense of responsibility within the National Committee.

In a sense, the National Committee is an agency with special purposes. Its position as a separate party organ is influenced by the absence of a party organ with more general purposes. Should there be such an organ, it would be conceivable that the National Committee eventually might best perform its functions as part of that organ or in close relationship to it.

3. *The Party Council.* One of the most serious problems in the present scheme of party organization is that of securing a proper measure of common understanding and harmony of action between the national, congressional and state organizations of the same party.

A solution requires, first, that some means be found for obtaining such cohesion within the congressional organization itself. As one aspect a sufficient degree of joint House and Senate organization is needed, instead of the present separate and independent party organizations for each house. A solution requires, secondly, that there be better machinery for White House liaison with the congressional organization on general legislative policy. It is necessary to provide appropriate consultation between the President and the leaders of his own party in Congress; to avoid the danger of putting the President in the role of the exclusive leader in respect to legislation; and to cultivate the idea that the party in power itself, rather than particular individuals at either end of Pennsylvania Avenue, is responsible for its record of legislative and executive action. Thus it will be easier to develop harmony and understanding, instead of jealousy and suspicion, between the President and Congress.

The particulars are matters for attention elsewhere in our report. What deserves emphasis here is the important point that somehow the congressional organization must maintain effective contact with the national organization of the party. With such contact it becomes much easier to avoid the friction and hostility so frequently observable; to build up a common understanding about the interpretation and application of the party platform; and in general to work toward a united party. Similarly, the present independent position of the state party organizations requires that some machinery or method be devised for promoting contact between these organizations themselves and between them and the national organization.

The pressing need for making the national, congressional and state organizations truly elements of one party can best be met by establishing a new agency within the national organization, perhaps to be known as the Party Council. Charles E. Merriam proposed such a Party Council thirty years ago.[2] He pointed out that while in some ways the party is overorganized, "on the side of organization for the consideration of party policies and party techniques it is singularly defective. The leaders, the managers and the responsible officials are not brought together for consultation as they would be in almost any other form of organization. They have neither the personal contact which is so valuable in all groups, the comparative study of management, nor the interchange of ideas regarding national or party policies, as in other groups."

It is a remarkable comment on the present structure of both major parties that such party leaders as Grover Cleveland, Theodore Roosevelt,

---

[2] See Charles E. Merriam, "Nomination of Presidential Candidates," *American Bar Association Journal*, Vol. 7, p. 83 (February, 1921), and Charles E. Merriam and Harold F. Gosnell, *The American Party System* (4th ed., New York 1949), pp. 356–60.

William Jennings Bryan, Woodrow Wilson, Charles E. Hughes, Herbert Hoover, Alfred E. Smith, Robert M. La Follette, William E. Borah, Wendell L. Willkie, Thomas E. Dewey and Franklin D. Roosevelt never held an official party position. They were therefore not entitled to participate formally in the consideration and determination of questions of party policy, strategy, management or organization.

Vigorous leaders, like Theodore Roosevelt, Woodrow Wilson and Franklin D. Roosevelt, did, of course, exercise great influence in respect to such matters, but largely because of their position and power as President. Yet even they held no title to a seat on their party's National Committee for the formal consideration of party business. Other leaders, such as Wendell L. Willkie and Thomas E. Dewey, though nominated by their party to the highest office in the country, had a most uncertain and ambiguous role in respect to Republican policies.

In other words, the system of party organization has drawn a rather sharp line. On the one side are those chosen by the party to manage its affairs. On the other side are those chosen by the party to carry out public policy, together with those others in neither party nor public office who are recognized throughout the country as outstanding leaders by virtue of their personality and qualities.

Professor Merriam therefore proposed that the Party Council be composed of five different groups: (1) the President, the Vice President, and the Cabinet of the majority party, and the leading presidential candidates at the previous presidential primaries for the minority party; (2) the party members in Congress; (3) the party's governors and their runners-up (that is, the defeated nominees); (4) the National Committeemen and state chairmen; and (5) prominent party leaders chosen by the National Committee or state committees, or by party leagues or associations, presumably such as the Young Democrats and Young Republicans.

This would make a Party Council of about 600-700 members, bringing together "the threads of party control and of leadership," in Professor Merriam's words. The council was expected to meet each year for the consideration of questions of party management and policy. It was to become an annual conference for acquaintance and consultation, and a forum and testing place for plans and personalities.

Professor Merriam's proposal was never adopted, but even before its presentation its basic principle was recognized and put into effect by the Republican party. The Republican National Committee, on December 10, 1919, actually created a Party Council called by that name. It was composed of 24 members, 12 of whom were members of the National Committee, and 12 were prominent outsiders, including four women. For each group, members were chosen who represented the various viewpoints and factional differences within the party.[3]

This Party Council was set up, according to the resolution of the National Committee, to deliberate on matters touching the party welfare; to make recommendations for the consideration of the National Committee and of the National Convention; and to consider subjects to be incorporated into the party platform. Clearly the council was also suited to serve as a link between the national, congressional and state organizations, since there were members connected with each. In addition, it presented a means of considering and perhaps reconciling any conflicting points of view on party policy, management and strategy. Although it was officially set up, there is no record of any confirmation of the Party Council by the National Convention, and it evidently ceased to function after a few years.

Reestablishment of some such Party Council, and in each party, would be a more constructive move today. If the idea was ahead of its time after World War I, subsequent conditions have certainly caught up with it. Professor Merriam's proposal has much to commend it, but what is now most needed is a body that can meet frequently, consult easily with other party agencies, deal with current party problems, and become a source of continuing advice to the President or, in the case of the minority party, to some other recognized party leader.

As much can be said to support the idea of a rather large gathering, so not a little can be said to justify a very small working group. The former would be less competent for consultation and coordination. The latter might be too small to gain the confidence of the party as a whole. Neither alternative fits the present needs and circumstances. The greatest need is for a body that can consult effectively. On the other hand, that body cannot afford to operate as a tight little cluster.

For reasons of general confidence, again, the Party Council should not be packed with people taking the national view of party affairs and policies. To pull together different interests, the council must allow these interests to enter.

---

[3] The following members were from the *National Committee:* H. O. Bursum (N. M.), W. H. Crocker (Calif.), R. B. Howell (Neb.), W. M. Crane (Mass.), V. L. Highland (W. Va.), H. F. McGregor (Tex.), Frank B. Kellogg (Minn.), Herbert Parsons (N. Y.), Reed Smoot (Utah), J. M. Moorhead (N. C.), Boies Penrose (Pa.), and C. B Warren (Mich). The following members sat as *outsiders:* Walter Brown (O.), George W. Perkins (N. Y.), Elihu Root (N. Y.), Henry L. Stimson (N. Y.), Mrs. Mary Gibson (Calif.), Mrs. John G. Smith (Ky.), E. Cullivan (Calif.), Raymond Robins (Ill.), Julius Rosenwald (Ill.), William Allen White (Kans.), Miss Mary G. Hay (N. Y.), and Mrs. Harriet T. Upton (O.).

We therefore *propose a Party Council of 50 members*, made up of representatives of five main groups: the National Committee (probably 5, chosen by the committee); the congressional party organization (5 from each house, chosen by the respective organization); the state committees (10, chosen on a regional basis by the regional groups, if any, otherwise by the National Convention); the party's governors (5, chosen by them); and other recognized party groups, such as the Young Republicans and Young Democrats, as well as the party following at large (20, with the majority chosen by the National Convention and the remainder by the particular groups). The President and Vice President, the nominees for these offices, the highest national party officials, and perhaps some Cabinet officers designated by the President ought to be considered ex-officio members and fully entitled to participate.

Obviously the President—and to a lesser extent the recognized leader of the other party—occupies a central place in a party organ as important as the council. Even if he does not always personally attend its meetings, he may often take the initiative in raising questions of policy and program. Ideally the council would be the most important link between the party of the President and his Administration in the governmental sense. There must be sensible give-and-take between both, on the basis of a party program which will have to be implemented by the Administration, Congress and the council.

Such a Party Council should consider and settle the larger problems of party management, within limits prescribed by the National Convention; propose a preliminary draft of the party platform to the National Convention; interpret the platform in relation to current problems; choose for the National Convention the group of party leaders outside the party organizations; consider and make recommendations to appropriate party organs in respect to congressional candidates; and make recommendations to the National Convention, the National Committee or other appropriate party organs with respect to conspicuous departures from general party decisions by state or local party organizations.

The Party Council should meet regularly and often, at least quarterly. It should draw into its discussions ideas about party policy from everywhere, and certainly never try to shut out any sources of policy influence in and out of government. It should make full reports of its transactions to the National Convention. *In presidential years, the council would naturally become a place for the discussion of presidential candidacies, and might well perform the useful function of screening these candidacies in a preliminary way.* It would, in a very real sense, be a "forum and testing place of plans and personalities," to quote once more Professor Merriam. On all these matters it is particularly important, as he put it, to bring together the threads of party control and party leadership. When that is done successfully, the council may well be able to demonstrate even to the hesitant that it can be a real factor in the tough business of winning elections.

Within this Party Council there might well be a smaller group of party advisers to the President—or, in the other party, to the presidential nominee or other recognized party leader—*to serve as a party cabinet.* The smaller group would consist of the highest party officials. These would include the permanent chairman of the National Convention, the chairman of the National Committee, the chairman of the Party Council, the chairman of the joint congressional caucus (if any), the floor leaders, and the Vice President and Speaker. Such a group, if established, should have a prominent position in all other national party organs; at any rate it should have the right to appear, to speak, to consult and to be consulted.

II. Intraparty Relationships

1. *State and Local Party Organizations. Organizational patterns of the parties are predicated on the assumption that a party committee is necessary for each electoral area. There is a growing dissatisfaction with the results of this system on the local level, especially the multiplicity of organizations.* One finds not only state and county central committees, but also a considerable number of congressional, judicial, probate, state senatorial and assembly district organizations, as well as city, village and township committees. The place of power within the local groups varies from state to state, and committee functions are seldom precisely defined. Some functions may be imposed by law, others outlined in the by-laws, and still others derived from custom.

In many if not most of the states, local party organization is confusing and sketchy, with party leaders themselves unclear on the lines of authority and relationships within and between the maze of committees. Some county and municipal committees have over a thousand members.[4] In practice, the plethora and composition of committees lend themselves to boss rule. As a result, prominent members of the party often shun positions on the party committees.

[4] Kings County (Brooklyn, N. Y.), for example, has a committee of over 2,500 members; four of the five counties in New York City exceed 1,600 persons. See Hugh A. Bone, "Political Parties in New York City," *American Political Science Review*, Vol. 40, p. 272 (April. 1946). Commenting upon party organization, the author writes: "New York City is composed of five counties or boroughs, without any formal city-wide party organization. Consequently, there are five autonomous and unrelated centers of control within a municipal party. . . . To complicate the situation, the rules for county organization differ from borough to borough, and few in the party have any clear conception of their own committee's rules, let alone those of the other counties." *Ibid.*, pp. 272–273.

This dispersion of ill-defined local party authority and the proliferation of committees and conventions seriously affect party responsibility. National party officials frequently are uncertain as to which local unit is the responsible one in terms of the presidential campaign, and oftentimes the real director of the party locally holds no position on the county or other local committee. Each committee campaigns for the officers in its district, and commonly fails to give much assistance to the national and state ticket. Very often no effective party organization is created to support the party's nominee for Congress. Because they are unable to receive financial and other help, candidates for Congress often look to private groups for assistance. This practice weakens the development of a strong congressional party, and enhances the influence of pressure groups in the lawmaking process.

An increasing number of state legislators are noting the breakdown or lack of party responsibility and discipline and the growth of internal separatism in state government. Most of the observations made elsewhere in this report about the inadequacy of the present party system, especially in Congress, apply with equal or more force to the state legislature. Although all but two states use the partisan ballot for the choice of members to the state legislature, the parties in many states fail to formulate a meaningful program to guide their representatives and to inform the voters.

County and municipal party organizations, to an even greater extent, fail to draft constructive policies for their nominees. Despite their great importance, the problems of metropolitan areas meet with almost a total lack of interest, partly because the boundaries of these areas are seldom coterminous with those of the local party units. Often there is no satisfactory liaison or system of intercommittee consultation.

It is necessary for both parties to reexamine their purposes and functions in the light of the present-day environment, state and local, in which they operate. Modernization of local party machinery in the interest of effective performance in this environment is long overdue. A reorientation of the leaders is needed from preoccupation with patronage and control of offices to interest in local, state, regional and national policies. Many county chairmen have failed to understand the reasons for the creation of competitive party associations and for the activities of organized labor's political action committees and such groups as the local units of Americans for Democratic Action. One of the main reasons is the dissatisfaction with the attitudes, purposes and operation of the official party organization.

One party leader, noting in his state "the lack of one official organization for party members to join and work with," thought that the National Committee should prepare a model plan for state organization.

In view of the strong tradition of autonomy, it is doubtful that the suggestion would be well received in many states. State and local party leaders, however, should reappraise their organization, methods and objectives in the interest of creating a higher degree of party responsibility in the state and the locality. Many of the proposals included in this report for improving national party institutions and party organization in Congress have relevance as a basis for a corresponding strengthening of party responsibility on the state and local levels.

2. *Relations between National, State and Local Organizations.* As has been previously pointed out, the state party organizations are not only independent of the national organization, but also independent of one another. This situation is probably the principal reason for the frequent difficulty, discord and confusion within the parties. The Republican party of California may take a position on public questions and even on party strategy very different from that of the Republican party of Iowa, and both may differ in these respects from the national organization.

Familiar examples are the differences and even hostility between the national Republican organization and the Wisconsin Republican organization during the period of La Follette control; between the national and the North Dakota Republican organizations, when the latter was dominated by the Nonpartisan League; and more recently between the national Democratic organization and the several southern state organizations controlled by the Dixiecrats. Many other examples could be given, where the differences are not so conspicuous but nevertheless seriously impede concerted party action.

The minor or third parties are generally organized in such a way as to ensure harmony within the party. They do not deny a measure of state autonomy in respect to decision and action, but see to it that decisions of the national bodies take precedence over conflicting state decisions. There can therefore be only one kind of basic party doctrine and policy—that determined by the national organization. The state and local organizations must conform to it.

Reorganization of the two major parties on the model of the minor or third parties in order to achieve the same ends appears neither desirable nor feasible. *Establishment of a Party Council, as here suggested, would do much to coordinate the different party organizations, and should be pressed with that objective in mind.*

Developments indicate that party leaders are now increasingly conscious of the necessity of cultivating closer working relationships between the various parts of the total party structure. In fact some progress has been made in that respect. Occasional meetings have been held during recent years of the state committee chairmen within a selected area, these meetings being usually attended also by the area members of the National Committee and its chairman. More recently *regional conferences* have been *held by both parties*, dealing with subjects of national as well as special interest within a region, and again attended by representatives of the National Committee and the state committees and by other party leaders. These conferences *have clearly been fruitful* in providing intimate and candid interchange of opinions, in cultivating good feeling, and in promoting understanding, harmony and common action within the area and at large.

Regional party organizations also are in the process of formation and *should be encouraged.* They may well become the means of both better representation in national organs and broader understanding of party problems and policies. Already there are indications of more formal and more frequent conferences between the National Committee and the responsible heads of the state committees to deal with questions of strategy as well as policy. The very desirable result is a more uniform party position in congressional, state and presidential campaigns.[5]

It is also highly important that the *local party organizations should be imbued with a stronger sense of loyalty to the entire party organization and feel their responsibility for promoting the broader policies of the party. This can be done by fostering local party meetings, regularly and frequently held, perhaps monthly.* Their purpose would be discussion of current and future party policy at all levels of government. From such meetings reports and recommendations should go to the Party Council. Local activity of this kind would make clear the views of the rank and file, and aid in discovering and bringing out good candidates for party and public office. Much would thus be gained for party unity and loyalty.[6]

[5] There is, for example, a formally organized Midwest Democratic Conference, whose governing board consists of the National Committeemen and the state chairmen and vice chairmen from the 13 states included in the conference. On February 16, 1950, a Democratic strategy conference was held in Washington, to which National Chairman Boyle invited the entire National Committee and the state chairmen and vice chairmen. A Republican policy or strategy committee was set up on the initiative of National Chairman Scott, consisting of representatives of the National Committee and the state committees, of the congressional organizations, and of the party's governors.

[6] The importance of local party meetings in promoting understanding, loyalty and unity in a party system organized, somewhat like ours, on the federal plan, is made clear by Louise Overacker in a recent study of the Australian Labor Party: "It is through the local party branch, successor to the 'leagues' of the 1890's, that opinion of the rank and file is made known to the leaders, and the rank and file is kept informed about the plans of the leaders. The biweekly branch meeting is an important sounding board, a 'party town meeting,' and a business unit. During an election campaign, it becomes a highly efficient campaign committee as well. These basic units are the nerve centers of the party, and their vitality largely determines the vitality of the party. . . . " Louise Overacker, "The Australian Labor Party," *American Political Science Review*, Vol. 43, pp. 677–703 (August, 1949), esp. p. 689.

As an ultimate remedy, unaffected by the legally independent status of the state party organizations, the national organization may exercise certain powers to bolster loyalty. By resorting to these powers *the national organization may deal with conspicuous or continued disloyalty on the part of any state organization.* The National Committee may exclude or expel disloyal members of that committee, and the National Convention may refuse to seat delegations on such grounds.

Although both bodies have on several occasions exercised these powers, *consideration should be given to the development of additional means of dealing with rebellious and disloyal state organizations.* Authoritative pronouncements by the Party Council and public appeal to the party membership affected may be such means. Use of party funds to replace the disloyal leadership of the state organization may be another. Still another might be appointment of temporary state officers, perhaps by the Party Council. One thing is entirely clear. It is contrary to the basic concept of our two-party system, destructive of party responsibility and disruptive of the party as a whole to permit organized disloyalty to continue.

3. *Headquarters and Staff.* Until recent years the organizations of the major parties were essentially only campaign organizations. They established headquarters, expanded their staffs, and operated at high speed during the campaign weeks, but virtually shut up shop during the intervening period. The National Committee, as the managing committee of the party, normally met only twice during its four-year term. The first meeting was held immediately after its election by the National Convention, for the purpose of choosing its officers and campaign committees. The second meeting took place in December or January preceding the next National Convention, for the purpose of issuing the call for that convention.

A member of the Democratic National Committee in 1919 described the situation in these words: "It was the custom of this body immediately after the Presidential election had passed—and the custom seems to prevail, whether we succeeded, as we did in Cleveland's time, or lost—of going out of business in a week or two, just as soon as we could pay up the bills, and indeed sometimes we went out of business before we did that."[7] Although some improvement had occurred since 1919, a close student of party methods was able to write as follows in 1944:

The usual American practice is a feverish construction of a party headquarters staff capable of real organization and propaganda service a few months

---

[7] Patrick H. Quinn (R. I.), at the meeting of the Democratic National Committee, February 26, 1919. *Proceedings, Democratic National Convention* (1920), p. 468.

before a presidential campaign. The skeleton gets flesh and bones on the eve of a national convention or soon after a nominee is chosen. After an election, the major part of a headquarters staff melts away. The waste and inefficiency of this procedure is in strong contrast to the permanent smooth-running machinery of a British organization. During campaigns a British party finds it necessary to add only a handful of paid employees, and its office expenses do not increase materially while the electioneering period is in progress.[8]

Permanent and continuous party organization apparently began about 1916 under the leadership of President Wilson. But it was not until Chairman John J. Raskob, of the Democratic National Committee, pressed the matter energetically, following the campaign of 1928, that an effective organization was actually set up to operate continuously. "I have reached the conclusion," he said in April 1929, after numerous conferences with National Committeemen and other party leaders, "that the party's interests can be advanced best by the opening of permanent and adequate headquarters in Washington and the conducting of active organization work 365 days in the year."

Thereafter a number of full-time, well-salaried officials were employed by the National Committee, the headquarters staff was expanded, and research and publicity activities were carried on continuously, though in a limited way. In 1932 Chairman Raskob even proposed at least annual meetings of the National Committee itself. "With meetings supposed to be held only every four years, the Chairman does not get the kind of cooperation that should be had from an organization representing the great Democratic Party in this country."[9]

Following the defeat of 1936, the Republican National Committee put Chairman John Hamilton on a full-time, salaried basis. He had previously suggested a more active and continuous organization, and even a four-year membership plan with regular dues to the party. In 1944 the Democrats provided the same arrangement for Chairman Robert E. Hannegan. After their defeat in 1944, the Republicans again gave atten-

---

[8] Ralph D. Casey, "British Politics—Some Lessons in Campaign Propaganda," *Public Opinion Quarterly*, Vol. 8, p. 74 (Spring, 1944); see also E. E. Schattschneider, "Party Government and Employment Policy," *American Political Science Review*, Vol. 39, p. 1155 (December, 1945). John Hamilton, while chairman of the Republican National Committee, visited the headquarters of the British Conservative Party in London and expressed great surprise at the "thoroughness and permanence of the organization." The Republican national headquarters staff was reduced from several hundred during the campaign of 1936 to about 40 after the election, and the Democratic staff from about 500 to 50–75.

[9] *Proceedings, Democratic National Convention* (1932), p. 469. A subcommittee of the Democratic National Committee was appointed to consider this proposal and others, but there is no record of its report. However, it is now understood that the chairman may call special meetings of the National Committee.

tion to the problem of a more effective organization. In 1945 they adopted an 8-point program proposed by Chairman Brownell.

This program called for: (1) a national organization to function on a full-time, all-year-round basis, with an enlarged and trained staff; (2) close working relations with the Senate and House party organizations; (3) staffs equipped for research, investigation and publicity to serve party members in Congress as well as the National Committee; (4) a vigorous program of cooperation of the National Committee with the House and Senate party members, the party's governors and state organizations; (5) integration of the activities of the National Committee with the activities of state and county committees; (6) more active participation by individual members of the National Committee in the development and execution of a party program; (7) a broadened basis for contributions to the party treasury; and (8) cooperation between the National Committee and the House and Senate organization in congressional campaigns.

This program has by no means been put into effect completely, but it represents a sound goal. *Both parties are now aware of the need to maintain permanent headquarters, with staffs equipped for research and publicity. A beginning has been made, but much still remains to be done.*

Staff development at party headquarters provides the essential mechanism to enable each party to concern itself appropriately with its continuing responsibilities. Availability of professionally trained staff, in particular, makes it more readily possible for the party leadership to grasp issues clearly, to see trends and problems in perspective, and to consider the far-flung interests of the party as a whole. Without adequate party staffs, leaders can hardly hope to cope with the complexity of party strategy and tactics in our day.

7. Party Platforms

To indicate how the party stands on the many interrelated issues that concern various parts of the electorate, to offer a coherent program, and to provide the voters with a proper choice between the alternative policies and programs advanced by the two parties, a careful formulation of each party's position is required. The party platform has a vital part to play in our party system.

I. Nature of the Platform

1. *Alternative purposes. Should the party platform be a statement of general principles representing the permanent or long-range philosophy of the party? Or should it state the party's position on immediate issues?*

Actually, the platform is usually made up of both the more permanent and the more fleeting elements.

Nor is it possible to state either principles or issues in such a way that application to immediate problems is clear beyond any further question. That is so because the circumstances and situations are constantly changing and cannot be completely foreseen when the platform is written, particularly in the case of the national platform, which is traditionally presented only quadrennially. It is also true that the platform may be intentionally written in an ambiguous manner so as to attract voters of any persuasion and to offend as few voters as possible. But when this ruse helps to put a party into office, it is equally likely to produce disappointment through lack of performance and in the end do the party little good.

2. *Interpretation of the Platform.* Even when honestly prepared, however, a platform requires interpretation in the details of its policies and the application of general principles to current problems. At present there is no agency within the party structure that has clear authority so to interpret and apply the platform. This condition gives rise to conflict and discord over the question of authority as well as over the actual position of the party on particular points.

Members of Congress commonly claim the right to determine the party position on matters of legislation, especially after the off-year elections. The National Committee sometimes attempts to interpret the platform, but finds its authority sharply challenged. The President can make such attempts with more success for the majority party, although certainly not with ease. For the minority party there is no one with the President's standing or power. This is one of the serious gaps in the party machinery, which would best be filled by the proposed Party Council. *As a body representing the various parts of the party structure, the Party Council should be able to give authoritative and reasonably acceptable interpretations of the platform.* Perhaps it could occasionally even make more specific or reformulate the party principles in their application to current situations.

3. *National-state Platform Conflicts.* Another problem in respect to the party platform arises out of the relationship between the national and state platforms. In view of the independent position of the state party organizations, the state party platform may and frequently does state principles and policies quite different from those stated in the national platform. Such divergencies make things confusing both for the party candidates from the state and for the public, and make nonsense of the party system.

What is needed is better coordination in the declaration of party principles. There is also need for an understanding, if not a formal regulation, that the national platform—as a representative document agreed to by the body of the party—is supreme in respect to general principles and national issues. This would still allow the state organizations considerable latitude in respect to purely state or local problems. *The Party Council would be the appropriate party agency to interpret the respective platforms and determine the right position in case of conflict.*

Would such authority to interpret in case of conflict lead to an undesirable enlargement of the national platform sphere? Strong tendencies that operate in the American party system run counter to this possibility. *There is very little likelihood indeed for the Party Council to be inconsiderate of arguable claims of state autonomy.*

4. *Binding Character.* A further problem is that of the extent to which the platform is or should be binding upon the party candidates. The idea underneath a platform certainly is that the party, when in power, intends to put the various planks into effect. This would imply that the party candidates are committed to the support of these planks. Probably no one would disagree with the recent statement of Senator Ives of New York on February 11, 1950, that "Unless party platform pledges are made with the solemn conviction that they shall be kept, the party responsible for them is deserving only of the hostile public reaction which disregard for them inevitably provokes."[1]

In addition to the implication, in the very nature of a platform, of a binding pledge to the public, the parties themselves have often included in the platform a solemn promise of fulfillment. For instance, the Democratic platform of 1932 gave this pledge:

We believe that a party platform is a covenant with the people to be faithfully kept by the party when entrusted with power, and that the people are entitled to know in plain words the terms of the contract to which they are asked to subscribe. . . . The Democratic Party solemnly promises by appropriate action to put into effect the principles, policies, and reforms herein advocated, and to eradicate the policies, methods, and practices herein condemned.

The Republicans in 1936, 1940 and 1944 incorporated the following pledge into their platform: "The acceptance of the nominations tendered by this Convention carries with it, as a matter of private honor and public faith, an undertaking by each candidate to be true to the principles and program herein set forth."

In spite of these clear implications and express pledges, there has been much difference of opinion as to the exact binding quality of a platform.

[1] Quoted in *New York Times*, February 17, 1950.

William Jennings Bryan took the position that a platform is completely binding on the party candidates, and that one who violates the platform is "worse than a criminal." By contrast, Senator Norris stated in respect to the St. Lawrence Waterway proposal that "I am entirely moved in my vote upon the treaty by my own convictions, and not in any degree by the platform of any political party, and I think such conviction ought to decide the question. But there are many men more able than I, and just as honest, who do not agree with me as to that, but who believe in the party system of settling such questions as this."

President Wilson argued, with regard to the Democratic platform of 1912, that the established party principles should be considered as more binding than any exceptional plank departing from them. Moreover, there is always the argument that new situations or conditions make the platform pledges less binding. Finally, the range of different matters has to be considered. The Democratic platform of 1928 put the point this way: "The function of a national platform is to declare principles and party policies. We do not, therefore, assume to bind our party respecting local issues or details of legislation."

All of this suggests the need for appropriate machinery, such as a Party Council, to interpret and apply the national platform in respect to doubts or details. When that is done by way of authoritative and continuing statement, the party program should be considered generally binding. It should be added, however, that our conclusion has for a starting point a platform responsibly formulated—that is, one reflecting ideas and promises behind which most of the party membership can line up. This differs from a platform dressed up to lure but not actually to satisfy particular groups of voters.

The generally binding effect of the party platform is particularly obvious in relation to the national (that is, presidential and congressional) candidates and officeholders. But state and local candidates and officeholders would be similarly bound, under the national as well as state and local platforms, with the Party Council seeking to remedy any troublesome discrepancies between the state and national platforms. Of course, such implicit commitment by party candidates and officeholders is neither intended to produce dead uniformity of individual action nor is it in fact ever without bounds. It would allow defined reservations similar to those permitted under the Democratic House Caucus Rules.

II. Problems of Platform-making

1. *Method of Formulating Party Platforms.* Much of the difficulty, confusion and difference of opinion with respect to the importance and

effectiveness of the party platform arises from the method of its formulation. The fact that the national and state platforms are separately framed and adopted makes possible the sharp divergencies that may appear within the same party. *Occasionally the state platforms are deliberately delayed until after the national platform has been adopted, in order to have a basis for conformity. Such practice is to be encouraged, and state legislation that prevents it ought to be changed.* To avoid conflict on the same questions, national platforms should be confined, so far as possible, to general principles and national issues, and state platforms to purely state and local issues.

Since adoption of the national platform is now closely associated with the nomination of presidential candidates only, there is additional difficulty, under the present method, of getting congressional candidates and members of Congress to respect it. This is particularly the case in off-year campaigns, which are entirely congressional campaigns and two years removed from the National Convention and the national platform.

"No Republican National Convention can be held to make any binding declarations regarding policy before next year's elections," said Senator Taft in 1941, "and the party National Committee clearly has no authority to make such declarations. I see no reason why each Congressman and each Senator should not run on his own foreign policy." *A method of platform-making that is closely related to the congressional as well as to the presidential campaign must* therefore *be developed, and with more direct participation by the party members of Congress.* These should feel that it is their platform as much as it is the President's.

The large and unwieldy platform committee, working in the dramatic and emotional circumstances of the traditional convention, ordinarily provides little real deliberation. The platform as an important statement of party principles and program is often not heard at all by many delegates, and the method of arriving at it is not conducive to responsible action.

2. *Improvement of Platforms and Platform-making.* The necessity of improving the method of platform-making has actually been recognized for many years. President Wilson, in 1913, proposed that the National Convention concentrate on adopting the platform. "Conventions," he said, "should determine nothing but party platforms and should be made up of the men who would be expected, if elected, to carry those platforms into effect." He therefore urged an ex-officio convention instead of one of delegates—a system which has, in fact, been established in some states under the primary laws.

The Republican National Committee, at the same time (in 1919) that it ventured to create the Party Council, also set up an Advisory Committee on Platform and Policies. This committee, consisting of 171 leading men and women in the party under the chairmanship of Ogden L. Mills, was provided with expert staff assistance in the persons of Professor Samuel McCune Lindsay of Columbia University and Professor Jacob H. Hollander of Johns Hopkins University. It divided itself into several subcommittees, which in turn prepared and circulated to about 75,000 persons detailed questionnaires on a dozen particular questions then currently important. On that basis the committee prepared a report for the Platform Committee of the National Convention.

A second committee relating to the platform was simultaneously set up, the Preliminary Committee on Platform. It consisted of 50 members, those twelve members of the National Committee who were also members of the Party Council and 38 outsiders. The function of this committee was to draft a tentative platform for final action by the convention committee, presumably using the materials and reports of the larger Advisory Committee. In explaining these developments, Mr. Will Hays, the Republican National Chairman, said that "If a party platform is to be a mere string of political platitudes, then it can easily be written in forty-eight hours. If it is to be a solemn declaration of a responsible party's real purposes, it deserves the most careful consideration." These devices for securing a better considered and more responsible platform were confirmed by the Republican Convention of 1920, and were kept in use for some time.

Other developments, also within the Republican Party, show concern with the problem of an effective statement of the principles and program. One might mention the Committee on Program, set up in 1937 under the chairmanship of President Glenn Frank of the University of Wisconsin; the Post-War Advisory Committee and the Mackinac Conference in 1944; and the recent Committee on Policy initiated by Chairman Scott and continued by Chairman Gabrielson.

In both parties, the Platform Committee or a working part of it is now appointed some weeks in advance of the National Convention. Thus the platform finally submitted to the convention is actually prepared with more care. The difficulty is that such advance actions are without authority, since the Platform Committee is a convention committee and not a general party committee. Hence the best that can be hoped for is that the advance arrangements will be later confirmed by the convention itself. In both parties also, *the practice of holding public hearings on the policies to be incorporated into the platform has been fairly well established.*

This consultation is of importance, for it makes the parties aware of the interest in particular policies. Here local party meetings can play another constructive role.

3. *Proposals.* Keeping in mind both the improved procedures already in course of development and the need for further improvement, we make the following proposals:

(a) *Party platforms,* and particularly national platforms, *should be formulated at least every two years,* in order to relate to current issues and provide a closer connection with the off-year congressional campaigns.

(b) *National platforms should emphasize general party principles and national issues,* and with respect to such principles and issues should be regarded as binding commitments on all candidates and officeholders of the party, national, state and local.

(c) *State and local platforms* should emphasize state and local issues, and *should be expected to conform to the national platform on matters of general party principle or on national policies.*

(d) *To achieve better machinery for platform-making, the Party Council, when set up, should prepare a tentative draft well in advance of the National Convention for the consideration of the appropriate convention committee and the convention itself.* Occasionally a thorough review of the party principles will be desirable, which might again be undertaken by the Party Council or by some special committee similar to those used in the past.

(e) *Local party meetings should be held* regularly and frequently *for the discussion and consideration of platform proposals.*

8. *Party Organization in Congress*

I. Introduction

1. *External Factors.* In Congress the two political parties are on almost daily trial. Each house is organized by its majority party. Both parties are represented on legislative, special and investigatorial committees. In Congress, party campaign promises are kept or broken, and reputations of party leaders are made or lost.

A higher degree of party responsibility in Congress cannot be provided merely by actions taken within Congress. The cohesiveness and morale of the congressional members of the party are inevitably affected by the activities of the party's National Convention, the party's National Committee and—in the case of the Administration party—the President. Above all, the basis of party operations in Congress is laid in the election process. Members of Congress, though elected as the candidates of one party, may be sharply divided on basic national issues, and particularly upon the programs called for in their party's national platform. Then little, if anything, can be done within Congress to heal the breach.

Nevertheless, at a time when there are signs on many fronts of a trend toward greater party responsibility,[1] *action within Congress can be of decisive significance.* It can accelerate the trend and reinforce efforts made elsewhere.

2. *Continuous Evolution.* Blueprints for the complete reconstruction of Congress are easy to draw—and have often been drawn. Yet complete reconstruction is not only utopian; it is also unnecessary. Moreover, *the materials for responsible party operations in Congress are already on hand. The key to progress lies in making a full-scale effort to use them.*

A general structure of congressional party organization already exists. It should be tightened up. The party leadership in both houses already has certain functions with respect to the handling of relations with the President and the shaping of the committee structure. These functions should be strengthened. It already has other functions with respect to the legislative schedule, which also should be strengthened.

If such action were taken, it would not mean that every issue would become a party issue. It would not eliminate the need for or the possibility of nonpartisan and bipartisan policies. But it would result in a more responsible approach to party programs and a more orderly handling of *all* congressional activities.

II. Tightening Up the Congressional Party Organization

Party organization is complex. It also varies from house to house and from party to party. For the sake of simplicity, however, it is here discussed in terms of the party leaders, the party leadership committees, and the party caucuses or conferences.

1. *The Leaders. For more than ten years now the press has carried news about regular meetings between the President and the Big Four of Congress —the Speaker of the House, the Majority Leader of the House, the Vice*

---

[1] The trend is also documented by general pressure for reform on the congressional level. As one example, the additional Heller report (National Committee for Strengthening Congress, under Robert Heller's chairmanship) of December 27, 1949, recommending further steps (*Congressional Record*, Vol. 96, pp. A164ff. [January 11, 1950]), also concerns itself with the need for increased party responsibility. The report (p. A166) suggests "more extensive use of the caucus as an instrument for the formation and promotion of party policy"; election by the caucus for two years of party policy committees "without regard to seniority"; collaboration between the two policy committees, in House and Senate, of the majority party in planning the legislative program; designation of chairmen and members of the standing committees by these party policy committees; insistence on willingness to carry out the party program as the basic requirement of chairmanship in a standing committee; and reconsideration of committee assignments about every two years "to allow the shifting of uncooperative members."

President and the Majority Leader of the Senate, when the four are of the President's party. Despite their informal character—or possibly because of it—these Big Four meetings have provided an essential tie between Congress and the executive branch. They have given the four congressional leaders an insight into the President's plans and a form of prestige that could not have otherwise been acquired. They have also given the President a valued link with Congress and an important source of guidance and counsel.

In view of the development of this tradition, *it would be an error to attempt to supplant the relationship between the Big Four and the President by some new body* to carry on the same function. An executive-legislative cabinet to provide another bridge between the Chief Executive and Congress would cut down the leadership position of the Big Four.[2]

Whenever it becomes necessary for the President to meet with the leaders of both parties in Congress, it is a simple matter for the Big Four to be expanded into six or eight. This, in fact, has occasionally been done in recent years. On bipartisan issues it should probably be done more frequently. The objective of developing a mechanism for consultation among the party leadership as a whole can best be met by the Party Council discussed in a previous section.

The selection of the Big Four is something that has implications for the entire party. In the case of the Vice President, there is broad party participation through the nominating convention and the election. A somewhat different form of participation is called for in the selection of the remaining three. Neither the Speaker of the House nor the two majority leaders can be regarded merely as representing the party members in the particular house. The same applies to the minority leaders in each house.

In the public eye a party leader like these is a spokesman for his party as a whole. It is necessary, therefore, *that there be broad consultation*

---

[2] The idea of a more formal advisory policy body joining together the legislative and executive branches has come up rather frequently in recent years. It is not a new idea, of course. Richard S. Childs, for example, who almost a generation back assumed a leading part in governmental reform, proposed some such arrangement to President Wilson in 1917. To quote Mr. Childs (*National Municipal Review*, Vol. 39, pp. 114–115 [February, 1950]), the proposal urged the President to "handpick from both houses of Congress an 'executive committee' of members who are congenial politically, territorially representative, experienced and possessed of some natural leadership in Congress." This committee would meet each week with the President. "Its members would stand high in Congress by virtue of the president's confidence and backing, their inside knowledge and their ability to command expert departmental help. They would formulate the budget and the legislative program, fight for 'administration measures' on the floor of Congress, and constitute an informal ministry." Wilson, according to Childs, called the proposal "thoroughly worth thinking about," but took no steps to act on it.

throughout the national leadership of a party before a party leader is elected in either house. In particular, this consultative process should include the party organization in both houses and the President.

2. *The Leadership Committees.* The basic trouble at present is not that there are no party leadership committees but that there are too many committees exercising various leadership functions.

Some of these committees are called policy committees, some steering committees, some committees on committees. In fact, the Democratic members of a major legislative committee in the House, the Committee on Ways and Means, serve as their party's committee on committees—an arrangement that invites some doubt about its effectiveness in either direction. The Republican Committee on Committees is made up of one member elected by each state delegation who votes in accordance with that delegation's strength. In the House, also, the Rules Committee carries on certain legislative traffic functions that in the Senate are handled by the policy or steering committees of the parties. There is further the recently created Joint Committee on the Economic Report, which was set up under the Employment Act of 1946. This committee is supposed to bring forth on March 1 of each year a report as a means of coordinating the various legislative committees on matters relating to the economic health and growth of the nation.

The proliferation of leadership committees means that in neither house of Congress is there a body of party leaders who have the power of managing party affairs in Congress and who therefore can be held accountable for it. The result is that many things are left undone or—what is just as bad—are done in a dictatorial manner by individual party leaders. Also, too great a burden is thrown on the overworked Big Four and the Senate and House minority leaders.

To offer a ready-made blueprint to the members of Congress would seem pretentious. However, *we do submit these proposals:*

(a) *In both the Senate and House, the various separate leadership groups should be consolidated into one truly effective and responsible leadership committee for each party.*

(b) *Each of these four committees should be responsible not only for submitting policy proposals to the party membership, but also for discharging certain functions with respect to the committee structure and the legislative schedule.*

Each of the four committees should be selected or come up for a vote of confidence no less often than every two years, with opportunity for earlier challenge by a sufficiently large body of party members in the house if the committee fails to reflect the party program.

Occasion must be found reasonably often for the leadership committees of each party in the two houses to meet together. This is the only way to discuss common problems of legislative policy. *Furthermore, the rival leadership committees in each house should meet together on a more regular basis.* This is the best way to discuss the legislative schedule. It is not suggested, of course, that the majority party take less seriously the responsibility inherent in its prerogative to schedule legislative business. What we suggest, rather, is that interparty contact in this matter may make responsible scheduling easier.

A case can also be made for the four leadership groups to meet on specific occasions. This would provide an orderly approach to the broadening of areas of agreement between the two parties and to the identification both of party issues and of issues on which no congressional party policy is needed. An obvious occasion for such joint meetings is the transmission of the President's principal annual messages to Congress—the State of the Union message, the economic report and the budget message.

Something of this sort is already presaged in the work of the Joint Committee on the Economic Report. It is no longer a question whether the President's proposals be the starting point of the legislative schedule. They already are. The problem is how to get these proposals responsibly handled. At present they are not.

One of the reasons is that the Joint Committee on the Economic Report is composed of members of Congress who, for the most part, have no formal responsibility for party leadership. No committee of Congress other than one comprising the official party leadership—including the chairmen of the key committees—can serve to coordinate the main policy decisions that arise in the diversified activities distributed over the committee system. This logic points to the need for having the membership of the Joint Committee on the Economic Report include the responsible leaders of both parties—a need recognized early by such leaders as Senator Murray and Senator Flanders.

Another way to approach the same end would be to have the four party leadership committees meet jointly at the beginning of every session as a Joint Committee on the President's Program. Such a committee could consider the entire program embodied in the President's three principal annual messages and furnish guidance to the general line of action on the part of the various legislative committees.

3. *Caucuses or Conferences.* Whether they be called caucuses or conferences, *more frequent meetings of the party membership in each house should be held.* Otherwise there can be no real discussion of party positions and no real participation in or check upon the decisions of the party leadership. Without such discussion and participation, efforts to make party operations more responsible will be futile.

There is no formula to tell how often a caucus or conference should be convened merely to discuss matters and how often it should be held for the purpose of voting upon a position binding on the members. Nor is it possible to prescribe in other than general terms either the conditions under which a party member may be released from abiding by a caucus decision or the consequences to be invoked upon those who disregard the decision without release.[3] Three points, however, are rather clear.

The first is that *a binding caucus decision on legislative policy should be used primarily to carry out the party's principles and program.* Such a decision should not be used merely to support the views of the President or of congressional party leaders when their views do not rest on stated party policy, except in exigencies affecting the public record of the party.

The second is that members who generally stand behind the party program should have reason to know that their service is appreciated by the party leadership. Rewarding party loyalty is a proper way of fostering party unity. On the other hand, *when members of Congress disregard a caucus decision taken in furtherance of national party policy, they should expect disapproval.* They should not expect to receive the same consideration in the assignment of committee posts or in the apportionment of patronage as those who have been loyal to party principles. Their conduct should be brought before the eyes of the public. Their voters are entitled to know about it.

The third is that *the party leadership committees should be responsible for calling more frequent caucuses or conferences and developing the agenda of points for discussion.*

III. Party Responsibility for Committee Structure

Congressional committees have aptly been called "little legislatures." The bulk of congressional work is done in committee. It is in the committees, therefore, that the parties are put to their highest test.

1. *Selection of Committee Chairmen.* One often hears the lament that the seniority system is bad for the country but that there is just no other way of selecting committee chairmen. But this puts the problem in the wrong way.

The problem is not one of abolishing seniority and then finding an alternative. It is one of mobilizing the power through which the party leadership can successfully use the seniority principle rather than have the seniority principle dominate Congress. Under conditions of party

[3] The Democratic House Caucus Rules provide that members may be released when they have grounds to consider the decision unconstitutional or when the decision collides with a member's previous campaign commitments or with instructions from his constituency.

responsibility, with greater clarity of the party's position and broader acceptance of it, deliberate use of the seniority principle for purposes of party unity would be the opposite to personal power exercised by a particular individual or a small clique.

Advancement within a committee on the basis of seniority makes sense, other things being equal. But *it is not playing the game fairly for party members who oppose the commitments in their party's platform to rely on seniority to carry them into committee chairmanships. Party leaders have compelling reason to prevent such a member from becoming chairman —and they are entirely free so to exert their influence.* A chairmanship, after all, is like the position of a quarterback on a football team. It should not be given to someone who refuses to be a part of the team or who might even carry the ball across the wrong goal line. Nor is it satisfactory for either party to find itself saddled with a large number of chairmen representative in their thinking of only one element in the party.[4]

An all-out use of this approach, however, would run up against certain present-day realities. As long as party dissidents succeed in getting elected to Congress, they may hold a balance-of-power position between the two parties. If attempts were made to dislodge them from positions of power they might have gained in their party, they would be able to throw the control of either house into the hands of the opposing party. *The task of party leaders, when confronted with revolt on the part of committee chairmen, is hence not easy. Obviously problems of this sort must be handled in the electoral process itself as well as in the congressional arena.* Yet these practical limitations are far from insuperable, especially by consistent effort and crystallization of party doctrine. Similar limitations impede action everywhere. If they were regarded as excuses for inaction, progress at any point would be impossible.

To make the obvious explicit, we are not arguing here or elsewhere for parties made up of yes-men. Dissent is not undesirable in itself. It can be wholesome and constructive when it operates on a common basis. We are arguing the need for that common basis. Defiance of that common basis destroys the opportunity for party responsibility.

2. *Assignment of Members to Committees.* The distribution of committee positions among new members is one of the most important functions of party leadership. *The slates of committee assignments should be drawn up by the party leadership committees and presented to the appropriate party caucuses for approval or modification.* This applies to special and joint committees as well as to legislative committees. Where the Vice

[4] It has been suggested to us that when the Republican party is in control of Congress, under the seniority rule an undue proportion of chairmanships goes to midwestern conservatives, while control by the Democratic party similarly favors the South.

President and the Speaker of the House are given statutory power to appoint committee members, they should accept the slates offered by each of the parties on such a basis.

The principle of having both parties represented on every legislative committee is a sound one. However, *there is nothing sound in having the party ratio on the committees always correspond closely to the party ratio in the house itself*, which may often mean almost as many committee positions for the minority as for the majority—such as six to seven. This gives individual members of the majority party the balance of power and invites chaos. The results undermine party responsibility.

Regardless of the general proportion of party membership in each house, the majority party in the house should have a comfortable margin of control within each committee. The same applies, for the same reasons, to subcommittees. Of course, in thus taking more direct committee responsibility the majority party will hardly close its eyes to the attitudes in the electorate. Always the majority party will have to think of the next election.

Although much is to be gained in the committee by continuity and experience, there is also an advantage in having a regular review of the committee structure. *Committee assignments* should not be regarded as permanent prerogatives. Personal competence and party loyalty should be valued more highly than seniority in assigning members to such major committees as those dealing with fiscal policy and foreign affairs. Previous decisions with respect to committee assignments *should be subjected to regular reexamination by the party caucus or conference with reasonable frequency*, at least every two years.

Adjustments of this kind would make it much easier for either party to come forth with a consistent legislative record. They would reduce greatly the present differences in point of view among different committees, thus giving Congress itself a large measure of unity. They would cause committees to stand less on their vested jurisdictional rights. They would finally cut down the waste of effort that results from the inclination of individual committees to act as small legislatures apart from Congress at large—as when a committee reopens an issue settled by Congress in the course of implementing the prior decision of Congress.

3. *Committee Staff.* *Staff assistance should be available to minority as well as majority members of a committee whenever they want it.* It should not be within the power of the majority, as it is now, to deny this assistance. The excellent work of the Legislative Reference Service of the Library of Congress should not be expected to take the place of the more intensive type of analysis best done by committee staffs.

Committee staff for members of both parties is essential to provide a basis for sound party operations. It also contributes to the needed minimum of occupational security for professional staff members. *Where all committee staff is controlled by the majority, a change in power threatens continuity of service.* Top-quality staff would generally not be available under such conditions.

IV. Party Responsibility for the Legislative Schedule

There is always more work before Congress than can be handled. Not all of the bills reported upon by committees can be taken up on the floor. Only a portion of the bills introduced can be examined at public hearings. One of the greatest defects in present congressional committees is the absence of a truly responsible approach toward the scheduling of what is to be handled and when. Here lies one of the greatest opportunities for party leadership.

1. *The Need for Scheduling.* Scheduling should include not only what measures are to be taken from the calendar for floor action but also the general scheduling of major hearings. *Schedules should be openly explained on the floor in advance.* They should apply to all issues, not just party issues.

No one but party leaders can do this job properly. Policy and steering functions are inseparable. *No committee should be in charge of legislative scheduling except the party leadership committee.*

2. *House Guidance of Legislative Traffic.* For some time up to quite recently, the Rules Committee has held decisive control over the legislative calendar in the House, without attempting to act as a program expediter of the dominant party. At the beginning of the 81st Congress, the rules of the House were changed by allowing committee chairmen to bypass the Rules Committee under certain circumstances. This was a step in the right direction in so far as it partially removed a roadblock in the path of more responsible party control of legislative traffic.

It was far from a wholly satisfactory solution, however. The power taken away from an irresponsible group that did not represent the leadership of the two parties was distributed among the committee chairmen. These, today, do not yet act as a group of responsible party leaders. To safeguard his party the Speaker of the House has been forced on many occasions to deny recognition to individual committee chairmen.

A more *democratic approach would be to substitute open party control for control by the Rules Committee or individual chairmen.* There are many ways to do this. An extreme measure would be to abolish the Rules Committee altogether and have its functions taken over by the leadership committees of the two parties. A more feasible solution would

probably be to shift the steering function from the Rules Committee to
the leadership committee of the majority party. It might also be feasible
to give the Speaker and the Majority Leader jointly the power to bypass
the Rules Committee after a given period of time has elapsed, and upon
sufficient showing of support from the membership of the majority
party.

3. *The Right to Vote in the Senate.* The present cloture rule goes so far
in giving individual Senators the right to speak that it interferes with
the right of the majority to vote. It is a serious obstacle to responsible
lawmaking.

*The present cloture rule should be amended. The best rule is one that
provides for majority cloture on all matters before the Senate.* This need not
interfere with the right of Senators to speak for a reasonable length of
time. There is no lack of proposals submitted in the Senate which would
hold off the cloture vote for a given number of days or until each Senator
has had an opportunity to speak for a reasonable time.

9. *Political Participation*

The individual voter may personally participate in politics in several
ways. As a member of a party, associated with others in one of its local
units, he may share in initiating the party's program, discuss issues, pick
the local unit's leadership, select representatives to party gatherings
in larger geographical areas, win support for his party, and engage in
house-to-house campaigning at election time. Also as a member of a
party, he may participate directly or indirectly in selecting its candidates for office. Finally, as a member of the larger body politic, as a
citizen, he is called upon to participate in the choice of legislative, executive and judicial officeholders when election day rolls around.

All these kinds of individual participation in politics bear directly
upon the character of the party system. When such participation is both
free and widespread, parties are more fully responsive to popular preferences. *Widespread political participation thus fosters responsibility as
well as democratic control in the conduct of party affairs and the pursuit of
party policies. A more responsible party system is intimately linked with
the general level as well as the forms of political participation.*

I. Intraparty Democracy

1. *Party Membership.* Party membership in the United States lacks
the explicit basis which is found in some other democracies, where members pay dues, formally accept the party's stated objectives, and may
run the risk of disciplinary action if they publicly oppose its program.
Even where such explicit basis is absent, however, it is the hope of ac-

complishing common aims that leads people to act together. The ver
idea of party implies an association of broadly like-minded votei
seeking to carry out common objectives through their elected represer
tatives.

To justify its existence a party so conceived must demonstrate it
capacity to direct the course of public policy in line with announce
programs. This, in turn, means that those who speak for the party mus
follow a unified course of action. Unity among leaders, however, is diff
cult if they speak for members with entirely different objectives and fur
damentally different ideas on public policy. The meaning of membershi
itself suggests that those who identify themselves with the group hav
something in common which they do not share with those outside it.

This is not to say that there ought to be a complete absence of diffei
ences of opinion within the party ranks. Especially in a large and divers
fied nation like the United States, different views must necessarily k
blended and harmonized within each of the major parties, and ends a
well as means be subject to constant reconsideration. On the other hanc
it is clear that differences of opinion should be resolved to the greate:
extent possible; that they should be resolved in terms of a genera
national viewpoint; and that the position of the party as a body shoul
be made plain.

Capacity for internal agreement, democratically arrived at, is
critical test for a party. It is a critical test because when there is n
such capacity, there is no capacity for positive action, and hence th
party becomes a hollow pretense. It is a test which can be met only
the party machinery affords the membership an opportunity to set th
course of the party and to control those who speak for it. This test ca
be met fully only where the membership accepts responsibility for crea
tive participation in shaping the party's program.

If internal disagreements are to be resolved along the lines of genera
rather than special interests, members of the party, whether they liv
in Maine or California, should be able to appreciate their *common* coi
cerns. They should be encouraged to think in terms of national issue
and a national program, rather than in terms of primarily local conside
ations. In a party organized on democratic lines and with a nation:
point of view, cohesion springs naturally from willingness to suppoi
aims which the member himself has helped to shape and has come t
accept. Such a party will seldom need to resort to the artificial disciplir
of obligations declared binding.

Fostering traditions and institutions which encourage the membe
ship to play a more active role in party affairs is a major task. If the ra
ideas for party programs bubble up from beneath rather than trick

down from above, the programs will come closer to expressing what is in the hearts and minds of the members. More general and wholehearted support of the party program will follow wider participation in the program's development.

An active membership, willing to assume responsibility for creative participation in party affairs, cannot be created overnight. But it is possible to aid in its development. The institution of a Party Council, for example, with its emphasis on a national program and continuous reconsideration of party policy in terms of current issues, will prompt party members to think more in terms of policy, less in terms of personalities.

Formulation of programs linking state and local issues to questions of national and international concern will help overcome unduly narrow views of party. It will tend to break down the patronage-nomination-election concept of party, which has dominated the thinking of most local party organizations in the past. *As stress is placed by the parties upon policy and the interrelationship of problems at various levels of government, association with a party should become interesting and attractive to many who hold aloof today.*

2. *Machinery of Intraparty Democracy.* Wider and more purposeful activity by the membership may be induced by changes in organization at both the top and the bottom of the party pyramid. A National Convention, broadly and directly representative of the rank and file of the party and meeting at least biennially, is essential to promote a sense of identity with the party throughout the membership as well as to settle internal differences fairly, harmoniously and democratically. The Party Council, as the party organ continuously in touch with the implementation of party policy, might well report regularly to the convention and make recommendations to it.

If the National Convention is to serve as the grand assembly of the party in which diverse viewpoints are compounded into a course of action, it must be nourished from below. To this end local party groups are needed that meet frequently to discuss and initiate policy. Such continuous discussion builds up an interest in issues among the rank and file, and the ideas generated by it, expressing the thinking at the grass roots, would make it easier for the Party Council to act as an organ of the party as a whole. The local groups could also operate as channels through which the Party Council would inform the membership of action taken or contemplated, and explain the reasons for it. The logic of this two-way communication suggests that the Party Council might well take under its wing an integrated publicity and research program, emphasizing national issues and the interrelationship of national, state and local matters.

The local groups here referred to should be different in composition and function from most of the existing local party committees. The existing committees generally look too much to patronage, nominations and elections; their attitude, by and large, is too much one of indifference toward issues. The failure of many county and city committees to pull for presidential and congressional candidates cannot be ignored. The ease with which labor groups and political leagues have moved into areas of activity in which local party committees once reigned supreme indicates the need for a new type of local organization with a new outlook. Once the new type of local organization takes hold—and the building blocks are there today for citizen groups to use—the traditional local party unit may have to come to terms with it. The outcome may be far different from the familiar conditions of the past.

There is thus much to the idea of local party leagues, playing a creative role in shaping the *national* program, and with activities integrated into the national party structure. Certainly such units would add to the vitality of the party and tend to make the individual members more enthusiastic supporters. Much of the energy and interest which is now dissipated in writing letters to individual congressmen and participating in numerous public-cause groups could readily be absorbed by the parties through local party groups of this sort.

The regional party conferences held by both parties during recent years are useful additions to the local and national units already described. Another approach is the formation, in the individual congressional district, of an advisory council, serving as a liaison committee between the congressman and his constituents.[1] This is an area in which experience and the ingenuity of those in the thick of the party battle are likely to point the way.

Channels for expressing the ideas of the members are pointless unless there are ideas to express. A continuous flow of challenging material from the national party organization to local and regional groups would

[1] An interesting example of such a "people's lobby" is the Congressional Council for the Second Massachusetts District inaugurated by Representative Foster Furcolo, as described by him. It serves the dual purpose of keeping the Representative in touch with a cross-section of opinion within his district, and keeping the voters in touch with the affairs of their government. Organized on "nonpartisan and nonpolitical lines," the council is made up of 45 members drawn from among local government officials, state legislators, trade union leaders, farmers, small businessmen, veterans, educators, newspapermen and housewives. Representative Furcolo maintains that a great advantage of the council is that he cannot be "lobbied" without the knowledge of the people of the district and that he is bound to get "all sides of the story" (for his own account of the plan, see *Congressional Record*, Vol. 95, Appendix, pp. A94–95 [January 10, 1949]). As another method of communication, some members of Congress make it a practice to send their constituents regular "newsletters," keeping them informed of developments in Congress.

stimulate fruitful discussion. This calls for the development by the parties of the functions of research, education and publicity, to which they have hitherto given so scant attention. The organization of a research and publicity division within a permanent secretariat attached to the Party Council would increase the prestige of that body and promote party cohesion, as well as bring about a more thoughtful approach to campaign issues.

3. *Toward a New Concept of Party Membership.* Party membership in this country has come to mean little in terms of allegiance to common principles or support of a national party program. It is not unusual to find less like-mindedness among those bearing the same party label than among some of these and those who fight their political battles under a different party banner.

The existing confusion was vividly underscored by former President Hoover in a recent speech: "If a man from the moon, who knew the essentials of representative government, came as a total stranger to the United States, he would say some obvious things within the first week or two. . . . He would say that in all this ideological tumult, if there cannot be a reasonably cohesive body of opinion in each major party, you are on a blind road where there is no authority in the ballot or in government."[2]

Party membership, in the eyes of many Americans, is a "some time," "some body," "some place" thing. The existing primary laws of most states define party membership in terms of support of party candidates rather than allegiance to a common program. While such tests reflect rather than cause the lack of party unity in terms of policy, their existence in the laws makes it difficult to inject new meaning into party membership.

Even without radical changes in the existing state primary laws, however, it is possible to move gradually in the direction of a different concept of party membership. *The existence of a national program, drafted at frequent intervals by a party convention both broadly representative and enjoying prestige, should make a great difference. It would prompt those who identify themselves as Republicans or Democrats to think in terms of support of that program, rather than in terms of personalities, patronage and local matters.*

Participation of the rank and file in local party groups that help to shape party policy should work in the same direction. Members of a party who have an opportunity to contribute to its program feel a stronger obligation to support it, and are more likely to insist that it

[2] Speech made before the American Newspaper Publishers Association, *New York Herald Tribune*, April 28, 1950.

be supported by those who speak for the party in legislative chambers. The development of a more program-conscious party membership may attract into party activity many who formerly stayed away, including public-spirited citizens with great experience and knowledge. It will thus be a factor in giving the parties a greater measure of intellectual leadership.

With increased unity within the party it is likely that party membership will be given a more explicit basis. Those who claim the right to participate in framing the party's program and selecting its candidates may be very willing to support its national program by the payment of regular dues. *Once machinery is established which gives the party member and his representative a share in framing the party's objectives, once there are safeguards against internal dictation by a few in positions of influence, members and representatives will feel readier to assume an obligation to support the program.*

Membership defined in these terms does not ask for mindless discipline enforced from above. It generates the self-discipline which stems from free identification with aims one helps to define. Concerted action in the name of the party cannot and should not eliminate the intransigence of the rebel who goes his own way, but it can and should avoid both casual challenge to an accepted line of action and the waste of bloated dissent.

II. Nominating Procedures

1. *United States Senator and Representative.* Members of Congress are national officers in the sense that they legislate for the entire nation and sit in the only legislative body which may claim to represent the general, national interest. But *nominations for United States Senator and Representative are governed largely by state laws that vary radically in their provisions. National regulation would overcome the disadvantages of so much variety. But one must face the practical objections to national regulation.* Aside from the possible contention that a constitutional amendment would be necessary before uniform, national rules could be introduced, there are certain other reasons for leaving "genius of place" in control in this case. It is an area in which traditions are firmly established; any move against them would encounter stiff opposition. Moreover, nominations to state and even local offices are sometimes made at the same time that nominations for United States Senator and Representative are made, and are subject to the same rules. Two different sets of regulations would add to the complexity of procedures already confusing to the voter.

In all but one state *the direct primary*—that is, selection of candidates at the polls—is now an established institution. In spite of recognized imperfections it should be retained. It is a useful weapon in the arsenal of intraparty democracy. No workable substitute has been found for it, and it *probably can be adapted to the needs of parties unified in terms of national policy.* The primary election laws of many states badly need improvement. Here, however, we must confine ourselves to suggesting the direction major changes should take.

The relative advantages of open and closed primaries are still hotly debated.[3] In an open primary the voter is not required to register his party affiliation ahead of time or to disclose it when he applies for a primary ballot. He receives the ballots of all parties, and in the secrecy of the polling booth makes his decision. Party affiliation is thus a "some time" thing which may be changed from primary to primary. In more than three-fourths of the states some variation of the closed primary is used, voters being required either to register their affiliation beforehand or to declare their affiliation, subject to challenge, when they apply for ballots at the primary.

Supporters of the open primary argue that it preserves the full secrecy of the ballot, prevents intimidation, and avoids disfranchising the independent voter, who is unwilling to declare himself a member of one party or the other. In support of the closed primary it is urged that party members should be willing to "stand up and be counted," that it prevents raids in terms of participation by members of other parties, and that it is impossible to develop party responsibility if nominations may be controlled by those with no continuing allegiance to the party.

Out of this confusion one thing is clear. No state has as yet found an entirely satisfactory test of party in terms of allegiance to policies rather than personalities. The lack of unity in ideas has played into the hands of advocates of the open primary. The question of open versus closed primaries needs to be reconsidered from the angle of strengthening rather than weakening party cohesion and responsibility.

The closed primary deserves preference because it is more readily compatible with the development of a responsible party system. However imperfectly the idea may have worked out in some instances, it tends to support the concept of the party as an association of like-minded people. On the other hand, *the open primary tends to destroy the concept of membership as the basis of party organization.*

Frequent attention to the party's national platform should underscore the program implications of nominations and alter the character of the primary contests. As national issues grow more important, and

[3] For a full discussion see *Model Direct Primary Election System*, prepared by Joseph P. Harris for the National Municipal League (1950).

the relation between nominees and program becomes more explicit, more Americans will look upon the badge of party as an honorable one. There will be less likelihood of continued resistance among independent voters to enrolling as party members. The closed primary already is the rule in more than three-fourths of the states. The weight of argument is on the conclusion that we can advance more rapidly toward greater party cohesion by extending the closed primary and at the same time gradually infusing new meaning into party membership.

It is difficult to see how this goal can be achieved if *cross filing* and the Washington blanket primary should become general. The present California legislation is a telling example. Under this law, it is possible for the same person to stand before the voters as both the Democratic and the Republican candidate for Congress—and many so campaign. In the 1950 primaries a number of incumbent legislators in fact led on both tickets. This condition *is bound to obscure program differences between the parties, and to eliminate any sense of real membership on the part of the rank and file.* Governor Earl Warren, after capturing the gubernatorial nomination of both major parties in 1946, spoke of the result revealingly as a victory for nonpartisanship. He could have called it breakdown of party.

The Washington blanket primary corrupts the meaning of party even further by permitting voters at the same primary to roam at will among the parties. The voter may, for example, support a Democrat for the nomination of United States Senator, and a Republican for that of Representative. Thus it is possible for a voter to consider himself both a Democrat and a Republican at one and the same moment. Such provisions are a barrier to the development of a program-conscious attitude among party members.

The formal or informal proposal of candidates by preprimary meetings of responsible party committees or party councils is a healthy development. The theory that underlies the public presentation of candidates with whom party bodies are ready to identify themselves has much appeal. Further experimentation with this kind of machinery is desirable. Such procedures would encourage responsible leadership at a point where it is badly needed. Moreover, as Professor Joseph P. Harris has ably argued, they might draw into public life candidates who are both well qualified and ready to act in support of agreed-upon programs.

Quite appropriately the Party Council might become a testing ground for candidates for United States Senator or Representative. As it gained respect and prestige, it might take the initiative in encouraging able people, in wholehearted agreement with the national program, to enter the race. In this sphere it might act informally and in cooperation with state bodies. The exact machinery is less important than the principle that it is proper for a nationally representative party organ to discuss possible nominees for offices which are of national rather than local concern.

The formal or informal proposal of candidates at preprimary gatherings should not preclude others from formally contesting the nominations in the primaries. The way should always be open to those who wished to challenge organization-endorsed candidates by filing the usual petitions or declarations of candidacy.

2. *Presidential Nomination.* The nomination of the President should be vested in a body broadly representative of various geographical areas and viewpoints. Clearly the nominee and the program are so closely related that the same body should adopt the platform and name the candidate. The development of a tradition of continuity of leadership, in both the winning and the losing party, has much to recommend it. In the unsuccessful party, however, it would be difficult to break down the strong feeling against retaining a defeated candidate as even titular head of the opposition.

In the smaller *National Convention* proposed earlier, *delegates representative of the party membership* would make up a majority. They *should be chosen by direct vote of the rank and file.* Canadian experience suggests that the direct election of delegates to this important national gathering would give it a healthy "grass roots" flavor and encourage national party unity.[4] As a majority of our states now select their delegates by state conventions rather than by direct vote of party members, introduction of direct election would necessitate amendments to the laws of many states. In electing these delegates it will be necessary to accept the existing definitions of party membership in the laws of the respective states. At the same time it will be possible to work toward a more satisfactory basis of membership.

The convention might exercise its important functions more effectively if alternative policies and possible nominees were indicated for it beforehand. As a body vested with responsibility for grand strategy and continuously in touch with the implementation of party policy, *the Party Council naturally would concern itself with platform plans and the relative claims of those who might be considered for presidential and vice presidential nominations.* Tentative platform proposals, available to local party groups in advance of the convention, would stimulate discussion of issues and give convention delegates a clearer idea of the views of

4 For a discussion of this and other Canadian procedures, see John W. Lederle, "National Conventions: Canada Shows the Way," *Southwestern Social Science Quarterly*, Vol. 25, pp. 118–133 (September, 1944).

the rank and file. Such preliminary groundwork by a responsible Party Council might eliminate much of the hidden trading and finessing of the "smoke-filled room."

In time it may be feasible and desirable to substitute a direct, national presidential primary for the indirect procedure of the convention. Such a change would presumably necessitate a constitutional amendment, giving Congress control of presidential nominating procedures.

III. Elections

1. *Election of the President. The present method of electing the President and Vice President* gives the entire electoral vote of a state to the party polling the larger number of popular votes. This *fosters the blight of one-party monopoly and results in concentration of campaign artillery in pivotal industrial states where minority groups hold the balance of power.* Little incentive exists therefore for either a Democrat or a Republican to vote in Georgia, for example; Republicans know their candidate has no chance, and Democrats are sure their candidate will carry the state before the ballots are cast.

In various areas of the country where it can be observed, the one-party system shows itself the product of several causes, but among these the Electoral College in its existing form is perhaps the most important. Its effect upon voting habits in southern one-party states has long been recognized, but the effect upon party organization has been less emphasized. It means that local Republican organizations are of little consequence, with the national organization making no bid for votes in this area; hence an effective opposition is lacking. The effect upon the Democratic party has been even more unfortunate. As active campaigning is unnecessary, the national organization has no excuse to enter the picture. So it is easier than it otherwise would be for individuals out of step with the party as a whole to dominate state and local organizations[5]. V. O. Key's notable study entitled *Southern Politics*[5] is full of examples of the destructive effect of the one-party system on party organization, and of the relation to that system of the present method of choosing the nation's chief executive.

In the persistent agitation for change in the Electoral College system stress should be placed both upon giving all sections of the country a real voice in electing the President and the Vice President and upon developing a two-party system in present one-party areas. A system which would reduce the one-party areas would be an important step in the direction of greater party responsibility. Strategically placed minorities in now pivotal states could hardly be said to lose actual bargaining influence. Rather, they would exchange dubious promises made them by elements within either party for commitments by the party as a whole.

[5] (New York, 1949).

2. *Term of Representative.* Viewed in the general line of this report, *it appears desirable to lengthen the term of Representatives to four years.* The present term is so short that a freshman member is involved in a campaign for renomination before he knows his job or has had much opportunity to prove his worth to his constituents or his party. A more important consideration is the possible effect upon party unity of synchronizing the terms of Representative and President.

If the elections for these offices always coincide, recurrent emphasis upon national issues would promote legislative-executive party solidarity. Independently, the same end would be approached by biennial statements of party policy and the activity of the Party Council.

3. *Campaign Funds.* Party unity and responsibility can be fostered through appropriate control of the collection and distribution of campaign funds. *Existing statutory limitations work toward a scattering of responsibility for the collecting of funds among a large number of independent party and nonparty committees.* The law on the subject, indeed, confuses the issue by suggesting that the problem is one of *volume* rather than of *sources* of financial support.

The law puts a $3,000,000 ceiling on what any one committee may spend in a calendar year, and a $5,000 limit on individual contributions. *Repeal of these restrictions would make it possible for a national body to assume more responsibility in the field of party finance.* Repeal would also be an honest recognition of the fact that in an era of expensive media of communication, such as radio and television, no national party committee could possibly do an effective job of bringing the issues before the voters with a $3,000,000 budget.

The situation might be improved in still another way by giving a specified measure of government assistance to the parties. This would reduce their dependence on private financial support and put them in a more equal competitive position. The Oregon publicity pamphlet distributed at public expense, the limited use of free mailing privileges accorded candidates in Britain, and the provisions for free radio time for each party in Britain and Canada are experiments which may serve as examples.

As a general proposition, *everything that makes the party system more meaningful to all voters leads incidentally to a broadening of the base of financial support of the parties.* This, in turn, carries with it a more responsible employment and control of political funds. Conversely, such broadening of the base of financial support is the best available means of checking the irresponsible power of the small minority of large contributors to party funds. As the parties attract more members the time may be reached when they can depend largely if not entirely upon membership dues for their funds.

4. *Apportionment and Redistricting.* The 1950 census reflects great

shifts in the distribution of population. *It is* therefore an appropriate *time to insist upon congressional districts approximately equal in population.*

It is a striking commentary upon American democracy that representation is extraordinarily unequal. For example, in the 81st Congress one member from Ohio represented a population of 163,000, while another presumably spoke for 698,000. If, after the 1950 census, Congress would require state legislatures to carry out the intent of the Constitution speedily and accurately, the House of Representatives would reflect party strength much more fairly and accurately.

IV. Barriers to Voting

It is only at the polls that a party can be held finally accountable for its promises and its deeds. And it is through the act of election to a greater extent than through anything else that more widespread popular participation may be achieved in the political process. Americans therefore have rightfully associated the growth of democracy with the extension of the suffrage.

To an important extent, the lack of adequate participation in the electoral process is the result of disappointment as well as inertia. More significant operation of the party system would create greater interest in voting. Unfortunately, there are many barriers that still stand today between the citizen and the polls.

1. *Registration.* In many states registration and voting procedures impose unnecessary burdens upon the voter. They tend to discourage the timid and the busy as well as the ignorant and the lazy. Mastery of the mysteries of the procedures is all too frequently limited to the political practitioner who uses it for his own selfish ends. *The system of permanent registration should be extended* to those areas where voters are still compelled to register at recurring intervals before they are allowed to vote

In addition, the public bodies supervising elections should themselves take the responsibility for registering the citizens in their area. This would not only help purge the lists of the deceased and those who have moved elsewhere, but would also result in an addition of probably millions of qualified citizens to the registration rolls.

Every year many citizens are disfranchised by residence requirements that discriminate against newcomers to the election district. Safeguarding the orderly identification of qualified voters is, of course, essential But within these limits, *properly qualified newcomers to an area should b permitted to register and vote without undue delay.* A residence requirement of two years in the state clearly exceeds these limits.

2. *Access to the Polls.* Many people are kept away from the poll

because of pressure of time. In 1947 Senator Warren Magnuson of Washington offered *legislation establishing* the first Tuesday after the first Monday in November in every even-numbered year as *National Election Day* and making this day a holiday. Enactment of such a measure *would in all probability bring to the polls large numbers of people who would otherwise never come.*

Holding elections on Saturdays or Sundays, when most wage earners are not at work, is a practice followed in some other democracies. Where this would not collide with religious traditions of the community, it *would probably also help to increase the size of the vote.*

In some communities the polls are not kept open for a sufficient number of hours to meet the convenience of all voters. *Adequate voting time should be provided by opening the booths in the earlier morning hours and keeping them open into the late evening hours.* The delays in counting that might result from the extension of voting hours can be overcome by the use of modern voting machines.

Experience in many communities has proved that provision can be made to allow people to vote who cannot come to the polls because they are ill or out of town. *There is room for much elaboration in laws governing absentee balloting.*

3. *Undemocratic Limitations.* In some states the vote is denied by poll-tax requirements, white primaries, educational qualifications, social pressure and other *intentionally limiting devices.* These *should be overcome by a combination of legal change and educational efforts.*

In addition, *action is indicated to extend the suffrage to the inhabitants of the District of Columbia.* Denial of the vote to the population of the national capital today cannot be based on sound reasons of general policy.

4. *The Short Ballot.* In most states, names on the ballot are not limited to officers who frame policy; too many officials are elected, from President down to county coroner and even dog-catcher. As he works his way down the ballot, the voter is likely to be overcome by his awareness of knowing too little about so many candidates. In this way the long ballot becomes another limitation upon effective voting.

Adoption of the short ballot has long been advocated to remove all but policy-making posts from the ballot and to reduce the burden on the voter. It *would* also *concentrate* his choice *on contests with program implications and thus shift* his *attention toward issues rather than personalities.*

10. *Research on Political Parties*

A fuller understanding of the present-day tendencies in the American system of politics requires considerable extension of research on political parties. This is not a matter of one coordinated research program, but of contributions fron various sources.

First, the appropriate government agencies should do a much better job of collecting and publishing basic figures and facts concerning elections and parties. Second, the parties themselves should develop their own research programs. Third, intensive research studies of the parties by professional students and intimate observers are needed.

In this report, as pointed out earlier, we are not speaking primarily to specialists in political science and students of the party system. To outline an adequate program of desirable research on political parties would be a technical as well as lengthy affair. All we intend to do here is to make some general suggestions.

I. Basic Facts and Figures

At present, basic facts and figures about elections and parties are gathered by governments in a sporadic, haphazard and incomplete manner. Although about 40 states publish annual blue books or other volumes on election statistics and governmental organization within their respective areas, the information thus provided is spotty.

Only a few of these official publications give information about local elections. In arrangement and content the published data defy comparison from state to state. Except for the official canvass of congressional and presidential elections by the Senate and House of Representatives, no federal agency has recently compiled such information. Moreover, there is practically no place to turn for the full story of party activities as evidenced in voting records, actions of party leadership committees, and operations of state party organizations. Finally, there is a great dearth of collections in which one would find the various regulations, both formal and informal, governing party organization and operations.

An adequate compilation of such information is an essential prerequisite for more effective research activities, either by the political parties or by professional students.

1. *Election Statistics.* To get better facts and figures the first thing *we propose* is *the publication of an election yearbook by the Bureau of the Census.*

This yearbook should furnish precise information on primary, final, special and run-off elections for federal, state, county and municipal offices, and votes upon proposals referred to the electorate by those governments. For each election included there should be given:

   (a) Names and party affiliations of all candidates.

   (b) Nature of proposals voted upon.

   (c) Total votes for each candidate and proposal, and the vote within each city and county for each office or proposal that covers a larger area.

In addition, state summaries, with county and municpial data, should show:

(d) Data on current elections, such as: number of offices to be filled; number of candidates for each office; in sample precincts, total number of candidates and proposals acted upon by the voter on one occasion; number of potential, registered and actual voters, and (where applicable) new registrants; and type of ballot used, with sample copies of ballots collected for the files.

(e) Supplemental information on organization of elections, such as: schedule of elections for the current and succeeding year; election officials; number of election precincts; maps of judicial, legislative or other districts not following county lines; changes in districts; and legal qualifications for voting.

(f) Background demographic and general economic data, such as: comparisons showing population growth; composition of population; percentage of industrial and agricultural population; and similar data.

(g) Historical data, according to priorities of importance and availability, probably published separately on a deferred schedule as circumstances permit.

(h) Complete bibliographies of election information already published in a form readily accessible in larger libraries.

Prompt publication is needed for the election yearbook. Current election data must be published before the next campaign starts or they will have lost a large part of their value. Multicopied preliminary reports, however, could present important data currently before final results are published in a printed volume.

The arrangement of the yearbook should probably be by states, which would be most useful for local purposes. *In addition, a summary booklet for presidential and congressional elections*, with historical material, *should be issued.*

Two major aids in obtaining data on elections are available in most states. They should be used for the yearbook. First, there are the political scientists in state universities and other institutions of learning or research who could act as special consultants on their respective states and sometimes assist in making arrangements for obtaining data otherwise difficult of access. Second, the state Secretaries of State or other authorized central state election officers should be encouraged to take over as much of the collection work as possible, thus acting for the Bureau of the Census as well as in their own interest.

Such arrangements would result in a large saving of time and money for the yearbook. They would also have the effect of promoting improvements in local practices about keeping election records and publishing results, as the central state office would have to obtain uniform data promptly and completely in accordance with nationally recognized standards. A cooperative system of making use of technical assistance and governmental agencies within the states would also lead to improved election organization, because officials and the public would become better informed about prevailing local procedures and alternative methods used in other states.

2. *Party Activities. Compilation and regular publication of information on party activities are no less urgently needed.* This undertaking should include a summary of all recorded votes of members of Congress, whether cast on the floor of the Senate and the House or in congressional committees. It should also include similar information concerning voting in state legislatures.

It is equally desirable to compile and publish the names of all the members of party leadership committees in Congress, of the national committees of the political parties and of the state committees, together with whatever public records can be obtained of meetings held and decisions made. In addition, a general analysis should be made of campaign expenditures by national, state and local party organizations. Much of the information obtained under the present laws requiring the registration of information on campaign expenditures is wasted because of lack of such analysis. A similar analysis of the information filed by lobbyists under existing legislation would serve public purposes, too. Buried data are data withheld.

The entire task is one that could be well performed by the Legislative Reference Service in the Library of Congress, with its specialized staff resources and its working contacts with both parties.

3. *Compilation of Party Regulations. A third task is the collection of all major regulations relating to national parties and elections.* These materials should include provisions of federal law, state law, party constitutions and party plans. It should also include an up-to-date compilation of laws relating to registration and primaries.

Because it is in character comparable to the gathering of information about party activities, this job could also best be done by the Legislative Reference Service of the Library of Congress.

II. More Research by the Parties

Research is a weapon. It is a weapon that is used for widely different purposes by pressure groups and by government agencies. It is a weapon that the parties should use more vigorously to plan sound programs, to stand up under bombardment by various interest groups, and to direct or criticize the government effectively.

1. *Party Research Staffs.* At the national level, party research staffs have generally been rather frail organs, expanded only before elections to collect facts and statistics for speeches. *What is needed is a much stronger full-time research organization, adequately financed and working on a year-in, year-out basis.*

A number of state party organizations have organized research staffs that have brought to the party leadership the intellectual resources of political scientists, economists and public administrators. This is an example that should be emulated not only by other state organizations but, above all, by the national organizations of the parties.

2. *Areas of Work. There are two fields of research that should always be of immediate interest to the national organization of every party.*

The first is the analysis of voting trends and voting behavior. The pioneering work done by Louis Bean in *How to Predict Elections*[1] is an example of the kind of analysis that each party might carry on for itself. When parties must invest increasingly large amounts in their appeal to the electorate, they ought to know much more precisely just how certain kinds and forms of appeals affect different bodies of voters. The application of social survey techniques to voting behavior is of equal significance.

A second research field is the analysis of various proposals dealing with changes in election methods. Any change—whether it be through congressional reapportionment, new regulations, court decisions or even proposed reforms of the Electoral College—creates new problems for party leadership or gives a different twist to old ones. Such problems have thus far been met by hunch rather than by careful analysis.

Research along these lines necessarily leads into problems of party policy and program. In the case of the opposition party, which finds it harder to gain access to the research resources of the executive branch, there is increased need for research on matters of public policy under the aegis of the national party organization.

Research also supplies a foundation for instruction among both party leaders and the rank and file. There seems to be a growing awareness on the part of some party leaders of the importance of knowledge built on research, particularly as an aid in the educational job of their party. The recent School of Politics sponsored by the Republican National Committee is a case in point. In June, 1950, the New York State Demo-

---

[1] (New York, 1948).

cratic Committee operated its fourth annual Political Institute on the campus of Colgate University. One of the authors of this report was asked in the summer of 1950 to set up a school for all Republican nominees and district leaders in an urban county, with some 70–100 in attendance for five weekly two-hour sessions. Schools of this kind have had successful forerunners, including the British party summer schools.

III. More Studies of the Parties

The study of political science has not stood still in recent years. But political parties as a subject of study have hardly found the emphasis they deserve. On balance, a greater degree of attention has been given during the past generation to governmental structure, functions and processes than to the broadly political phase of American life.

More research on political parties is needed both to fill noticeable gaps in the knowledge of society and to sustain and strengthen the research work that is being done in related fields.

1. *Types of Research Needed. In a field in which much still remains to be done, specific priorities have little meaning. The basic need is for a combination of creative hypotheses and realistic investigations.* There are opportunities for original ventures in methods of analysis as well as in questions to be pursued.

Fresh approaches will pay dividends in both the theory of political parties and the description of how they actually operate. A splendid example of the kind of research needed here is V. O. Key's *Southern Politics.*[2] What Professor Key has done for 11 southern states might well be done for the remaining 37 states.

But research by itself is not enough. Where research discloses defects in the operations of our parties, it is pertinent to inquire into appropriate methods of overcoming these defects. Writers on political parties have often found it difficult to assume this responsibility because it is one thing to diagnose and another to prescribe. Yet nothing is gained by keeping away from proposals for remedial action.

2. *Professors and Politics.* Since most professional research on political parties will be done in our colleges and universities, *the character of political research cannot be dissociated from the general approach of academic institutions to politics as a whole.* Generally speaking, these institutions have stressed the virtues of civic participation in the community but in the main preferred such participation not too close to the campus itself.

The subject of citizenship training by American colleges and universities has been discussed many times in the past. Persistent inadequacies have recently been summarized afresh in a report prepared for the Citizenship Clearing House at New York University by Thomas H. and

[2] (New York, 1949).

Doris D. Reed (February, 1950). One recommendation—agreed upon in the regional conferences held by the Clearing House and published with the report—is here particularly relevant. It calls for "faculty participation in the political scene."

In justification of this recommendation, the publication says:

Associations like the American Bar Association, the American Political Science Association and other national professional organizations might assist in overcoming the resistance in certain educational institutions to the introduction of practical courses in politics. Specifically, they could render great services by encouraging college trustees and presidents to permit political clubs on their campuses and by urging that professors be allowed to participate actively in the political scene as analysts or better yet as practitioners and that guest lecturers including practical politicians be permitted to partake in and enrich the courses in politics.[8]

As direct participants in the political process, teachers of political science on the whole have not made the contribution one might have hoped for in view of the value of their specialized knowledge. *Increased faculty participation in political affairs*, in turn, *would mean more practical, realistic and useful teaching as well as research in the field of political parties*. This is of particular importance in providing the conditions for a deeper understanding and a better operation of our party system. Too little is being done in universities and colleges to train future political leaders—national, state and local—who will be able to develop further the skills and techniques of the political process. New thought should be given to organized training programs for political leadership, utilizing the apprenticeship idea; for such programs financial support from the private foundations will be needed.

In brief, both teaching and research in political science need reorientation. The country is short of young men and women ready to rise to influential roles in the nation through effective participation in politics. There is also something of a shortage of scientifically tested knowledge about political behavior on which rising political leaders could freely rely.

3. *Role of Research Foundations.* Private foundations have been helpful in supporting research in the field of political parties. It is still true, nevertheless, that too small a proportion of foundation funds goes to this field. *The private foundations should actively solicit new ideas and proposals for research on political parties.*

Legislation has been pending for some time in Congress for a National Science Research Foundation. If this foundation is set up, it may well have indirectly or directly a stimulating effect also upon research in the social sciences, even though its main concern would be the physical

[8] P. 60.

sciences. Should direct support be forthcoming for areas of political science, it is to be hoped that party research will be given proper recognition.

4. *Role of American Political Science Association. The presentation of this report is but one instance of the interest shown in the subject of political parties by the American Political Science Association.*

The Association does not take a stand on documents of this kind, but has accepted our report as the judgment of a group of students. The purpose of the report is accomplished as it contributes to widespread debate of the American two-party system both inside and outside the profession. Such public discussion must provide the basis for constructive efforts by party leaders, who not only need to see their own way but also want to feel the support they are gaining within their party and in the general public for their moves toward refashioning party structure and procedure.

In addition, reports like ours, though in no way research documents in the ordinary sense, may serve as calls for research not yet undertaken. There are many members of the American Political Science Association who possess special competence to embark upon research projects devoted to political parties. *In making specific suggestions for the kinds of research projects that today appear most promising in this field, the Association could exert a further welcome influence.*

PART III. THE PROSPECT FOR ACTION

11. *Sources of Support and Leadership*

Readjustments in the structure and operation of the political parties, such as those here proposed, are in the nature of institutional change. Most of these readjustments will not require legislation or any other process of formal enactment. Rather, if they are to come at all, they must result from the growth of supporting opinion. They *call for a widespread appreciation, by influential parts of the public as well as by political leaders and party officials, of the kinds of change that are needed in order to bring about a more responsible operation of our two-party system.* The writing of this report will have been in vain unless the necessary support and leadership are available to bring forth a sufficiently widespread appreciation of the needed change.

Such support and leadership must be found among the groups and the influential individuals that make up the active political forces of the country. Each of these active political forces will have to examine its own position on the matter of a more effective party system. Hence it is worthwhile to review the main elements in the body politic to discover where they may be expected to stand. Perhaps we shall find that the forces of inertia and of opposition are not as great as may be thought.

1. *The Economic Pressure Groups.* If responsible party action is an alternative to government by pressure groups, will the pressure groups oppose change?

Obviously some of them will—particularly those that fear any kind of program based on popular preference and are opposed to having government so organized that it can formulate and carry out such programs. By definition these groups would be groups accustomed to achieve their ends by means other than action based on membership strength. The groups most likely to be in opposition are those *highly organized special interests with small or no direct voting power* which find their main stock in trade in the bad features of the present situation. Such groups *are best satisfied if the individual legislator and administrative official are kept defenseless in the face of their special pressure.* Fundamentally, the groups in this category hold an antidemocratic position.

Organizations with large membership are not in the same category. There are many such organizations, especially in agriculture, in labor and also in business. These organizations today find the public looking over their shoulders, as it were. Even if they wished less attention, they would be unable to escape it. They know that the demands they make upon the parties must at least appear justifiable to large numbers of voters. In other words, organizational demands increasingly tend to

85

be so formulated as to fit into a more broadly inclusive party program. In turn, the scope of its success in the political arena is being explained to its members by each large-membership organization in terms of the need for compromise with other interests indicated by the party program.

On balance, the large-membership groups should have little to fear, even as interest groups, from responsible party operations. Probably all of them could find points of gain among the proposals of this report. The question of where they will stand as organizations on the broad issue, however, is one that does not lend itself to easy prediction.

Any one of the large-membership organizations may be expected to oppose expressions of party responsibility in particular tactical situations where it finds itself in opposition to the program under which the majority party is trying to operate. Such situations will doubtless recur from time to time. They will inevitably tend to confuse views and weaken loyalties on the problem of a responsible party system as such.

Nevertheless, *it is reasonable to expect that those large-membership organizations with wise leadership will generally support the turn toward more responsible parties.* This will be true especially where either or both of two conditions exist. First, it will be true when the organization feels that it can effectively identify itself with a major part of the electorate, and can thus expect to be recognized in the program of one or the other party. Second, it will be true when the organization is prepared to come to terms with other groups whose interests may be different, and feels that such terms can be worked out more effectively within an improved party structure.

Moreover, any national organization whose members identify themselves mainly with one major political party has special reason for being favorable to more responsible planning and control within the party. The members themselves are likely to clamor for it and the organization has a vital interest in dependable party commitments.

In short, responsible parties may not be desired by special-interest groups that live on concentrated influence in the legislative and administrative spheres rather than on voting strength. But the broader the base and the more general the interests of the group, the more likely is the group to be favorable to party responsibility.

2. *The Party Leaders.* If such responsibility at the national level requires a strengthening of the national party leadership, will state and local leaders oppose it?

Some of them undoubtedly will, especially local *leaders who represent divergent sectional or other special interests within each party.* Again, however, it seems clear that this group is in the minority in each of the two parties, although some members of the group occupy positions of power. They *will look with disfavor upon any reforms that hit specifically at their personal vested interests.* But this group could be more than offset by the opposing groups in each party who frequently have helplessly watched as the interests of the national party were disregarded with damaging results in their own local situations.

State and local leaders often differ from national leaders of their own party in their responsiveness to national problems, particularly problems that do not have a visible local impact. Such local leaders may be reluctant to see a strengthening of the party's national organization. One answer is intensification of political education within each party. Certainly it is necessary for each national party headquarters to outline emerging national problems with sufficient precision for local party workers, so that all may understand the issues that arise and the necessity for national party action.

The greatest stake of party leaders at all levels is in the winning of elections. Ability to win elections is linked to the party's ability both to arrive at a program that will appeal to a majority of the electorate and to convince the electorate that the program will be carried out. For this reason many party leaders are interested in achieving an organization that would make the parties better fitted for responsibility in government.

This is particularly true of the party officials who hold national party office without occupying a governmental position with its separate interests. Virtually every chairman of a national party committee over the past decades has found grounds for complaint in the situation as it existed, and many of them have striven to do something about it. In the past they have had only limited support either from the public or within the parties. Yet their efforts have led to the first steps toward strengthening the position of the national party headquarters.

Most of the forward-looking leaders in each party are convinced that changes should be made. Many of them may welcome proposals for party reorganization. To some these will be an inducement to come up with effective suggestions of their own.

3. *The Government Officialdom.* If responsible parties are an alternative to government by bureaucracy, will the officialdom oppose it? Would such opposition make any difference?

To take the second question first, the answer is that it could make some difference, but not much. The influence of the administrative officialdom exists, but it is of a specialized character, and it is least potent of all on matters of internal party organization and operation.

Even the higher officials who carry some measure of political responsibility are subject to marked limitations on their effectiveness in party affairs.

On the first question, some administrative officials do find their interests closely linked today with certain special-interest groups. But this is largely the direct result of the absence of a good basis of support for a party program which means what it says. On the other hand, officials who work in agencies with strong program interests are among those who would most like to see fuller political responsibility at the top levels. They are the ones who inevitably must identify themselves with popular preferences and who are most strongly affected when these preferences fail to bring about a coherent governmental program.

To the extent that one may talk of government by bureaucracy, it exists because the officialdom has had to fill a vacuum. The vacuum arises precisely because the parties as parties have not been prepared to take responsibility for coming forward with national programs. Hence *greater program responsibility at the level of the political parties is likely to appeal to administrators and the career officialdom.* Certainly the stabilizing effects of party responsibility would in general run parallel to the basic interests of responsible officials in the executive agencies.

4. *Congress.* Will Congress willingly become a factor in support of party responsibility?

The balance of forces and the orientation of the leadership in the national parties is different from that in the congressional party organizations of the same label. In Congress, party organization has favored the "safe districts" of each party, which reflect a one-party system devoid of free competition. On the other hand, the national parties have found that they cannot win national elections with presidential candidates from one-party states or with platforms that have little appeal to the electorate in the two-party states.

As long as Congress gives most of the powerful committee chairmanships to members from the one-party districts and states, the interests of the congressional leadership of each party will show divergencies from those of the national parties and of the electorate as a whole. *It therefore cannot be expected that all* of the *congressional leaders*—particularly the senior committee chairmen with divergent sectional or other interests—*will be sympathetic to the concept of party responsibility.*

Each Congress, however, includes a large number of individual members from two-party districts, some very influential in their own right. Many of the outstanding members of Congress in each house are the product of political competition. In some instances, they are able to acquire enough seniority to reach positions of real power within Congress.

These members can become rallying points for the rank and file when the formal leadership is unsatisfactory, and their effectiveness *as leaders of national opinion* is particularly noteworthy. Such *influential members of each party in Congress can give strong support to the idea of party responsibility.* They can pull together large groups within each house, in the national parties and in the electorate generally.

5. *The President.* What is the stake of the President and of candidates for that office in the invigoration of our party system?

The President in office at any given time *can probably be more influential than any other single individual in attaining a better organized majority party, and thus also prompting the minority party to follow suit.* This is a problem of which no President has been entirely oblivious and to which many of them have given acute attention.

· The President occupies a triple position. As chief of state he is expected to rise above the level of party claims and obligations. As party head he is expected to lead the party along lines that will increase its capacity for securing and carrying out a popular program. As an individual in a post of great responsibility, he may well feel that he should have personal power commensurate with what he takes to be his responsibility.

It is clear that any President or candidate for the presidency who intends to work consistently and continuously in the direction of party responsibility may have to be prepared to share responsibility with other truly representative leaders of the party in the shaping of the party's program. He must also be prepared to use the party and its leaders in the process of policy-formulation.

The President could gain much when party leaders in and out of Congress are working together with him closely in matters concerning the party program. As party head, the President could then expect more widespread and more consistent support from the congressional leaders of his party. These, in turn, would present a more united front. As a result, on issues where the party as a party could be expected to have a program, the program of the party, of the party leaders in each house of Congress, and of the President would be the same program, not four different programs.

This general objective requires that the party's program organs become not only stronger but also more representative in a national sense. Here the President and the congressional leaders can exert decisive influence. *With greater party responsibility, the President's position as party leader would correspond in strength to the greater strength of his party*, and he would be far less in need of going his own way.

Situations will remain, of course, where the President must accept an unshared responsibility both as chief of state and in raising issues of national importance. But on all those broad questions on which in the end it is necessary to appeal to the electorate for support, the President cannot safely dissociate himself from his role as party head in seeking timely counsel with his party.

6. *The Electorate.* Is the electorate a political force so far as the achievement of party responsibility is concerned? If so, where will it stand?

The electorate in the large has always the power to give and the power to take away. On occasion it uses that power decisively. Considered as the total body of citizens to whom both party and governmental spokesmen appeal, *the electorate consists of three main groups: (1) those who seldom or never vote; (2) those who vote regularly for the party of their traditional affiliation; and (3) those who base their electoral choice upon the political performance of the two parties, as indicated by the programs they support and the candidates they succeed in putting forward.*

The first group is clearly no source of support to effect needed change. But it is likely to turn into a source of reward for those who promote such change successfully. Nonvoters can be converted into voters when they become sufficiently convinced that voting is important, which in turn depends upon whether a real choice is presented on matters they personally consider important.

The second group contributes to some extent to the inertia of the body politic, but it does include substantial numbers of citizens who take a continuing interest in the decisions of their party. In each major party, many members can be expected to favor change in the direction of a more responsible conduct of party affairs. Moreover, *the rank and file in each party want their party so organized that the views of the party majority will be respected and carried out.* Only thus can the parties remain confident of continuing support from their following.

The third group, made up of the active but less than wholly committed voters, is usually the deciding factor in elections wherever the two-party system functions effectively. This is the group that enables the electorate to choose between the two parties and to replace one with the other when the voters so decide.

Of these three groups, the first is virtually leaderless. The second finds its leadership mainly in officeholders or candidates for party or governmental office. The third group is assiduously courted by political leaders of all ranks, most of all by the President and by candidates for that office. It finds its own distinct leadership in all of the places, high and low, from which opinion develops.

In the end, *it may well be the members of the third group, in making their choices at election time, who will decide the question of our country's progress in the direction of a more responsible party system.*

Undoubtedly this group has mixed feelings on the issue. Characteristically, it tends to applaud the mavericks in each party when those mavericks show courage, honesty and devotion to the public good. Measures of party discipline have so far found relatively little support from these elements of the electorate in their capacity as keepers of the public conscience.

Such reactions rest in part on the well-founded conviction' that the parties have not been sufficiently responsive to the broad interests of the electorate or of their own membership; that party programs have frequently resulted from processes insufficiently representative to merit enforcement of commitments; and that party discipline has often been used without regard for a responsibly formulated program, and hence for the wrong reasons, or at the wrong times, or toward the wrong people.

These reasons for reluctance toward proposals for stronger party machinery would be in large part removed if the parties became more representative, more program-minded, and more concerned with winning the electorate on issues rather than personalities. Again it is the third group and their leaders that feel most strongly that the present situation is seriously deficient. It is this group that is willing to make an electoral choice and wants a choice to make; that wants to vote for a program and resents not having it carried out. *It is this group that occupies a place of critical importance in supporting a party system able to shoulder national responsibility.*

12. *The Dangers of Inaction*

Support for needed change comes from understanding of the change needed. If the case for change is conclusive, it makes no sense to ignore it stubbornly. In particular, it makes no sense to insist that there is always some risk in effecting changes, for the eventual outcome may not entirely conform to expectations. This result, no doubt, is possible, but it can be averted by appraising new experience while it is gained in observing the changes initiated. To magnify the risk of change out of proportion is to urge equally or more risky inertia. Doing nothing is no help when something ought to be done.

As the preceding section indicates, making the two parties better fitted to carry responsibility for the general line of national policy is an undertaking in which many hands must share. The motivation for sharing in this undertaking will not be exactly the same in each case. Expected benefits will differ in particulars, depending on the vantage point of each group and each individual playing a part in building a more effective party system. But one strand of reason is common to all of those participating in the effort. All will acknowledge the value of a party system that serves the basic interests of our country in its healthy domestic growth and its international security.

Today this is not a goal to be attended to at leisure, with unhurried step, as time permits. Time, on the contrary, intensifies the pressure for readjustments designed to build a stronger two-party system.

We have looked in one direction in order to find out what sources of support and leadership there are to bring about a strengthened party system. Now, at the end, we should also take a look in the other direction in order to find out how safely the country can wait before starting with the job. What are the dangers in doing nothing? How great are the dangers?

Anything as close to the vital process of representative government as the party system is bound to affect the nation's political life in more than one way. Whatever impairs the essential operation of the party system also produces serious difficulties in other spheres of national existence. Inaction in the face of needed change in this central area therefore increases the dangers which may be present.

Four of these *dangers warrant special emphasis. The first danger is that the inadequacy of the party system in sustaining well-considered programs and providing broad public support for them may lead to grave consequences in an explosive era. The second danger is that the American people may go too far for the safety of constitutional government in compensating for this inadequacy by shifting excessive responsibility to the President. The third danger is that with growing public cynicism and continuing proof of the ineffectiveness of the party system the nation may eventually witness the disintegration of the two major parties. The fourth danger is that the incapacity of the two parties for consistent action based on meaningful programs may rally support for extremist parties poles apart, each fanatically bent on imposing on the country its particular panacea.*

1. *The Danger of an Explosive Era.* Since the end of World War II, Americans have been enjoying a precarious and peculiar peace—peace of a sort. They are accustomed to talking about Two Worlds, with East and West facing each other. In this situation they have come to admit reluctantly not only that the United States must be on its guard but also that its national security must be commensurate with the realities of modern warfare. This means new ventures and new goals in planned

utilization of all our great resources, financial, diplomatic, military, productive, educational, psychological. The degree of needed coordination of these resources for national ends in itself does not pose an unattainable task. *But the political foundation of appropriate governmental programs is very unstable when it is not supplied by responsible party action.*

The same is true with respect to our domestic welfare proper. The Employment Act of 1946 expressed this country's new policy to take care actively that the economy remain on a high level of employment and production. Congress decided that the new policy could not be supported by any single legislative or administrative device but would have to be carried out by coordinated measures in many different fields of governmental activity. Again the necessary political basis can only be furnished by parties committed to programs. Should we ever tumble into a serious economic crisis for lack of such a firm basis, the loss of stature as well as strength may well prove a turning point for freedom throughout the world.

2. *The Danger of Overextending the Presidency.* The presidency is the greatest political office in this country. There is no other republic, in fact, that entrusts to its President as much constitutional responsibility as Americans have entrusted to the President of the United States.

He is the Chief Executive, and as such in command not only of the civilian departments of the Federal Government but also of the whole military establishment. His executive authority puts at his disposal all the administrative resources—in management, fact-finding, analysis and planning—that are available in the departmental system. By making authoritative legislative proposals and exercising his veto power, the President under the Constitution has a significant share in the work of Congress. In addition, he is the central figure in the leadership of his party, in and out of Congress.

It is still more important, perhaps, that the President is the only politically responsible organ of government that has the whole nation as constituency. Elected by the people at large, the President must look upon himself as its spokesman. In him alone all Americans find a single voice in national affairs.

It is therefore a natural tendency that time and again governmental responsibility for formulation of coherent programs and unity of action has been placed upon the President. He has been charged with the preparation of the annual budget—the work plan of the Federal Government that goes to Congress for review and final determination. He has also been charged with the presentation of the government's economic program, submitted to Congress in the periodic economic reports of the

President. He cannot relinquish the burden of establishing the general lines of American foreign policy. He has been charged with the development of coordinated policies to safeguard the country's national security.

In each of these large areas, the President is called upon to prepare the ground, to initiate the process of program formulation, to come forth with proposed programs for which he is prepared to assume political responsibility. As a result, Congress has the benefit of prior effort and concrete recommendations. This division of functions reflects a sound formula, evolved in practical experience. But to apply it effectively, somewhere *dependable political support has to be built up for the governmental program* as finally adopted. *When there is no other place to get that done, when the political parties fail to do it, it is tempting* once more *to turn to the President.*

But the President has no magic wand. If he acts in pursuit of a broad program that has been democratically formulated in his party, nearly all of his party is likely to put itself behind the measures called for by the program. Then the question of political support presents no difficulties, which is the solution suggested in this report. Lacking his party's support for a broad program, the President is left with only one course. He can attempt to fill the void caused by the absence of an effective party program by working up a broad political program of his own.

If he does, however, he has to go out and build the necessary support for that program through his personal effort without benefit of party. There are people who say that this is a realistic way of getting somewhere with good political ideas, especially ideas bound to leave cool both Congress and the larger part of the President's party. Some others say that the scheme is not the happiest thing but the only one practically available under presidential-congressional government.

Yet can there be much doubt about the ultimate implications? *When the President's program actually is the sole program* in this sense, *either his party becomes a flock of sheep or the party falls apart. In effect this concept of the presidency disposes of the party system by making the President reach directly for the support of a majority of the voters.* It favors a President who exploits skillfully the arts of demagoguery, who uses the whole country as his political backyard, and who does not mind turning into the embodiment of personal government.

A generation ago one might have dismissed this prospect as fantastic. At the midway mark of the twentieth century the American people has reason to know better, from recent and current examples abroad, what it does not want. Because Americans are so sure on that score, they cannot afford to be casual about overextending the presidency to the point where it might very well ring in the wrong ending.

3. *The Danger of Disintegration of the Two Parties.* It is a thing both familiar and deeply disturbing that many Americans have only caustic words or disdainful shrugs of the shoulder for the party system as it operates today. This attitude is a provocative comment on American democracy as a realistic proposition. With the national agenda crowded with problems and issues of great import, with the need for effective political processes to act on this agenda growing more urgent than ever, how can the two-party system in its present form survive repeated demonstrations of ineffectiveness and widespread public disaffection? How can the two parties hope to go on?

A chance that the electorate will turn its back upon the two parties is by no means academic. As a matter of fact, this development has already occurred in considerable part, and it is still going on. Present conditions are a great incentive for the voters to dispose of the parties as intermediaries between themselves and the government. In a way, a sizable body of the electorate has shifted from hopeful interest in the parties to the opposite attitude. This mass of voters sees itself as the President's or his opponent's direct electoral support.

Continued alienation between increasing numbers of voters and both major parties is an ominous tendency. It has a splintering effect and may lead to a system of several smaller parties. *American political institutions are too firmly grounded upon the two-party system to make its collapse a small matter.*

4. *The Danger of an Unbridgeable Political Cleavage. If the two parties do not develop alternative programs that can be executed, the voter's frustration and the mounting ambiguities of national policy might also set in motion more extreme tendencies to the political left and the political right.* This, again, would represent a condition to which neither our political institutions nor our civic habits are adapted. *Once a deep political cleavage develops between opposing groups, each group naturally works to keep it deep.* Such groups may gravitate beyond the confines of the American system of government and its democratic institutions.

Assuming a survival of the two-party system in form though not in spirit, even if only one of the diametrically opposite parties comes to flirt with unconstitutional means and ends, the consequences would be serious. For then the constitution-minded electorate would be virtually reduced to a one-party system with no practical alternative to holding to the "safe" party at all cost. The other party would not mind pushing the government into innovations in the political process from which there might be no return. Granting that the majority of the electorate showed no taste for such innovations, the large probability would remain that the constitutional party might grow fat and lazy on the assurance of continued support. A spoiled party could not measure up to the strain of our times.

Orientation of the American two-party system along the lines of meaningful national programs, far from producing an unhealthy cleavage dividing the electorate, *is* actually *a significant step toward avoiding the development of such a cleavage.* It is a way of keeping differences within bounds. It is a way of reinforcing the constitutional framework within which the voter may without peril exercise his freedom of political choice.

INDEX

A

Absentee voting, 77
Advisory bodies, local, *see* Parties, local organization
Agriculture, *see* Interest groups
American Political Science Association, 84
Apportionment, *see* Elections

B

Barriers to voting, *see* Elections
Bean, Louis, 81
Borah, Senator, 41; quoted, 27
Brownell, Republican National Committee Chairman, 50
Bryan, William J., 41; quoted, 53
Budget and Accounting Act, 32
Bureau of Internal Revenue, quoted, 32
Bureaucracy, *see* Officialdom
Business, *see* Interest groups

C

Cabinet, *see* President
Cabinet system, 35 ff.
California, 72
Canada, 73, 75
Candidacies, congressional, 21 ff., 24, 43, 45, 50, 53 ff., 68, 70 ff.; presidential, 43, 53 ff., 68, 73 ff.
Campaign committees, 29
Campaign funds, 45, 50, 70, 75, 80
Casey, Ralph D., quoted, 48–49
Caucus, *see* Parties, congressional organization
Census Bureau, 31, 78 ff.
Citizenship Clearing House, 82–83
Civic participation, *see* Parties, membership
Civic training, 82 ff.
Cleveland, Grover, 40
Cloture, *see* Legislative schedule
Coalition, 19
Committees, *see* Parties, congressional organization
Congressional party organization, *see* Parties
Convention, National, 28 ff., 37 ff., 54 ff., 67, 69, 73 ff.
Cross filing, *see* Primaries

D

Democratic party, 25, 28, 37, 49 ff., 52 ff., 55 ff., 74, 81–82

Dewey, Thomas E., 41
Discipline, 20 ff., 23 ff., 43, 48, 52 ff., 61 ff., 66 ff., 69 ff., 91

E

Election yearbook, 78 ff.
Elections, 74 ff., 80 ff.
Electoral College, *see* Elections
Electorate, and party responsibility, 90 ff., 95–96
Employment Act, 32, 59, 93
Executive-legislative cabinet, 58

F

Federalism, 26 ff.
Flanders, Senator, 60
Foundations, 83
Frank, Glenn, 55

G

Gabrielson, Republican National Committee Chairman, 55
Gaus, John M., quoted, 26
Georgia, 74
Great Britain, 35, 49, 75, 82

H

Hamilton, John, 49
Hannegan, Robert E., 49
Harris, Joseph P., 72
Hays, Will, quoted, 55
Holcombe, Arthur N., 33
Hollander, Jacob H., 55
Hoover, Herbert, 41; quoted, 69
Hughes, Charles E., 41

I

Ideological division, 20 ff., 92, 95–96
Illinois, 39
Interest groups, 19 ff., 31, 34 ff., 45, 68, 75, 85 ff., 88
Ives, Senator, quoted, 52

K

Key, V. O., 74, 82

L

Labor, *see* Interest groups
La Follette, Robert M., 41, 46
Legislative Reference Service, 63, 80
Legislative Reorganization Act, 32
Legislative schedule, 64 ff.

CPSIA information can be obtained
at www.ICGtesting.com
Printed in the USA
LVOW04s1742021216

515533LV00009B/734/P